# A PLEA FOR MAN

# A PLEA FOR MAN

*by*

MARIO M. ROSSI

EDINBURGH
AT THE UNIVERSITY PRESS
1956

PUBLISHED IN THE U. S. A. BY
ESSENTIAL BOOKS, INC.
FAIR LAWN,    NEW JERSEY

THE EDINBURGH UNIVERSITY PRESS

*Agents*

THOMAS NELSON AND SONS LTD
Parkside Works Edinburgh 9
36 Park Street London W1
312 Flinders Street Melbourne C1
218 Grand Parade Centre Cape Town

THOMAS NELSON AND SONS
19 East 47th Street New York 17

THOMAS NELSON AND SONS (CANADA) LTD
91-93 Wellington Street West Toronto 1

SOCIÉTÉ FRANÇAISE D'EDITIONS NELSON
25 rue Henri Barbusse Paris Vᵉ

To the memory
of
THEODOR LESSING

# CONTENTS

# CHAPTER I

# DID HISTORY HAPPEN?

We recognize only one science—the science of history.

> MARX (in *Marx-Engels Archiv*, I)

Man is a microcosm, not in a physical sense but in a historical sense, because he is a summary of universal history.

> CROCE, *History as Thought and Action*

Outside history, man is nothing.

> MUSSOLINI, *Doctrine of Fascism*

One learns from history itself even its application to actual needs. Whoever is incapable of this, cannot presume to be a political Führer.

> HITLER, *Mein Kampf*

ANCIENT TYRANTS pretended they had been sent by God to keep the populace in order, and the believer bowed to them as to a manifestation of God's will or to a divine scourge. In later times, during and after the Renaissance, a rougher sort of tyrants proclaimed that they had the might, and that might is right—or a good substitute for it. The tyrant did not need God's help. He helped himself. His rule was sanctioned by his own ability to gain power and to keep it in his hands.

The modern dictator, on the other hand, is helped to power by historians who maintain that history is basic reality and ultimate truth. According to them, if in a country, at a particular moment, a man is able by fair means or foul to gain absolute power, this means that tyranny was the unavoidable result of historical forces. The right of the dictator cannot be disputed since it is proved by his being there, by the emergence of his power in the course of history. To deny the right of the tyrant would be to ignore historical reality, which produces law and right.

This boundless faith in its value has given rise to several conceptions of the import of history. *Historical relativism* maintains that values of every kind (moral values, right and wrong, even religion) are related to a certain moment of history and lose their significance when that moment has passed. *Philosophy of history* avers that all events, all facts, are only manifestations of the development of some underlying reality which is always changing and becoming. Wars and philosophies, religions and literature, are bubbles rising to the surface of a dark river which streams everlastingly towards eternity—whether the stream be the dialectical 'becoming' of Hegel's 'Idea' or of Marx's technical conditions of production. *Historical positivism* on the other hand does

2

not accept a philosophical interpretation of history. It maintains that any historical event* is real in and by itself, and that you cannot go beyond it. There are not two realities—a deep-lying, innermost reality and its manifestation in historical events. There are no wheels within wheels in history. Any event is real. Historical knowledge of what happened is absolutely true. But we can speak of 'historicism'† in general as embracing these three conceptions in their common assumption of history as ultimate reality and of historical description as supreme science.

Before the end of the 17th century no historian dared claim a privileged position for history. Historians had, indeed, always attempted to elicit what really happened, and to order their facts in a reasonable and persuasive sequence: but 'history' meant description, narration, no more than a detailing of ordered facts, as opposed to science (or philosophy) which tried to explain, to find causes and reasons for them. 'Natural history' was a collection of natural facts; 'literary history' was an account of writers and their writings; 'civil history' or history proper described human actions in a certain period and place, or in the whole world. Historians, in ancient times, were, first and foremost, artists. They tried to set down facts with accuracy and evidence, in well-chosen words. Aristotle maintained in his *Rhetorics* that the historical style must needs be the most noble and elaborate.

Historical narration implies a previous procedure of another order. As it is impossible to detail all human events, the historian must choose the most important.

---

* We intend to use the term 'event' in its current meaning of historical happening, notwithstanding Whitehead's legitimate use of it to mean empirical occurrence, 'hard facts' as known to our immediate perception and considered as scientific evidence. For these last, we will use the term 'fact'.

† *Historizismus* in German includes any theory which attributes a historical nature to facts or forces of any kind.

While this choice does not depend, as in the case of poetry or fiction, upon artistic reasons, it too implies some rule or principle. The order to be given to events is governed by their relative position in time, but their connection does not depend upon their temporal sequence only. Many facts all happen before a certain historical event and any of them might be considered historically connected to it. A choice must therefore be made. The choice of certain facts to be described as the most important because of their influence on the course of events, is due in the last analysis to the tastes and beliefs and feelings of the historian. Therefore ancient writers concluded that history could not be a scientific description of absolute reality. They believed that its nature was rather that of pleading. Cicero for example who, as a great barrister, knew something about partial pleading and artistic harangues, considered history as a branch of the oratorical art, *opus oratorium maxime.*

The Christian, in turn, believed that behind any apparent fact lay a deeper purpose of the Almighty. But this deeper meaning of history was concealed from human eyes. A man could see only facts as they happened one by one, each one due to God. Any apparent connection between different historical events was a human connection; therefore it was not the real reason and cause of events. Only when God chose to reveal His purpose directly (as in the history of the Jews, told in the Bible) could we know something about the real aim, purpose, and structure of human events. For each set of events there were two histories—human history and the 'history of Providence'. Bacon considered the history of Providence as a science connected with Revelation. On this dual history Bossuet based his conception of universal history.

St. Augustine had already set forth a history of Providence when he tried to account for the decadence and dissolution of the Roman Empire. The history of Rome was, to human eyes, a glorious sequence of mighty men and of heroic deeds: but when confronted with the teaching of the Gospel it appeared only as a cavalcade of splendid vices, of brilliant crimes. Since one could not understand why God had allowed them to happen, and Rome to prosper, the real significance of Roman history could only be the working out of God's ultimate purpose, i.e. the diffusion of the Gospel.

What we call 'history' (wrote St. Augustine) teaches about the course of past times, but in fact it is useful only in so far as it helps to explain the Scriptures. Outside the Church, history is only childish erudition.

It would take too long to explain how this sober conception of history was superseded by History with a capital H, by history considered as supreme wisdom and the judge of men and nations, as counsel for the defence of evil deeds and criminals, of turncoats and dictators. The emergence of historicism was due to the limited outlook of those who forgot both the work of the historian in choosing facts, and the hand of Providence in producing them.

The first man to be guilty of this was a strange genius of the 18th century, Giambattista Vico, an Italian of budding fancy and specialized erudition in law and ancient history. His one-sided culture made him incapable of understanding scientific methods. He believed that science considered two quite different sets of notions as absolutely true—facts as attested by direct experience and truths as proved by logical reasoning. Since facts could not be explained but by God's unknown will, and truths, though elicited by our reason, lacked factual evidence, neither knowledge of nature (physical science) nor mathematics could be perfect sciences.

Turning then to historical facts (as Croce puts it) Vico felt he was capturing more intimately something he already possessed. ... He reconstructed human history, and what was human history but a production of man himself? And the human spirit which produces history, what is it but the same spirit which thinks and knows history?

In this way historical events in and by themselves appeared to Vico to be absolute knowledge—the only perfect knowledge given to man, since they are both truths and facts, perfectly known because the historian understands by direct knowledge the human mind which is the ultimate cause of human events, and experimentally evident because historical events—languages, literature, laws, wars, etc.—are 'hard facts'.

If, however, events reflected permanent peculiarities of the human mind, the same events should have appeared again and again. No change, no development or course of events would be possible if mankind remained always the same. Therefore the human mind must change. Vico claimed that it passed through three different stages. Each civilization, he said, begins with the dawn of the mind in a certain 'nation' or race (the Persian, the Greek, the Roman) and at first produces ways of living and expressions which reflect a childish, irrational turn of mind. Then mind advances from phantasy to reason, from poetry to prose, from religion to law. At last the civilization of that 'nation' disintegrates in a general decay of its peculiar spirit. Barbarism returns 'recurs' again, till a new 'nation' arises and passes again through the same three stages as did all former civilizations.

Now, asked Vico, why did every civilization stop and decay instead of going on and on towards ever higher forms of thought? Why did each 'nation' follow the same parabola? Whence this 'universal law of nations' which limits the extent of history and the scope of the human mind?

Vico was a good Christian, and was unwilling to assume that man might progress indefinitely, for if so the mind of man would have been potentially infinite and man himself would have been God in the making. Providence must be there, over and above history, curbing the progress of man. History was a perfect science, man could know perfectly mankind's doings—but both man and history were bound to a wheel turned by the invisible finger of God's 'uncontrollable intent'.

The theory was brilliant but inconsistent. Thinkers who accepted Vico's 'new science' were obliged to discard many of its elements in order to give logical plausibility to this historicism. They had to renounce the idea that Providence directed the general course of history, and deny that mankind proceeded in recurring cycles. In the end Vico's religious philosophy of history was cut out by his modern interpreters who accepted historicism in a broad sense only, and denied that any event has a motivation or meaning 'beyond itself'. Each event is absolute fact and absolute truth. To live and to write history are the same. There are no general *reasons* underlying the process of history. History goes on simply because man changes, and man changes because he passes through a succession of events.

Such is contemporary historicism, a sceptical conception of man and his destiny which offers the widest scope to anybody who wants to be 'tactful', to change his mind for a consideration and to sell his soul to a totalitarian regime. Historicism denies eternal truth, everlasting laws of conduct, everlasting God. No philosophy, no religion, it claims, can teach ultimate truth. Man thinks as he thinks because he has passed through a certain series of happenings which at any particular moment must result in a peculiar kind of religion or morals. On the other hand, historical events are what they are because they are expressions or 'positions' of a certain stage in mankind's course. No further reason, no further cause can or should be asked for.

Such disheartening, depraving consequences as these derive immediately from Vico's initial mistake in assuming that events are realities immediately known to us.

and that, since they are created by men like ourselves, we can know why and how they were produced. This implies that the mind of any man in the past and the mind of the historian are basically alike if not the same, that the mind of man never changes in its essentials. Now, if every historical event, every form of civilization owes its peculiarities to the peculiarities of the mind which brought it forth; if history is a course of different events and not just an everlasting repetition of the same, identical events, the human mind must be always changing, always evolving, and its change and evolution must be very deep indeed if its creations at a certain stage, at a certain moment, are quite different from those of another moment.

This is an evident inconsistency—and yet it is the very starting-point of Vico and of modern historicism. The absurdity becomes evident when we enquire deeper into the historical methods of Vico.

Vico assumed that it is possible for us to distinguish three stages in the history of any civilization, involving a change from an imaginative stage, in which man cannot reason but thinks and expresses himself in images and poetry, to a rational stage in which he creates laws. Do we, however, really *know* how the primitive mind, similar to that of children and savages, thinks? Our knowledge of it is the result of an arbitrary deduction, and not of intuitive evidence due to the fact that the minds of the primitive and of their historian are basically the same. Were the assumptions of Vico true, then any one particular sort of mind could reproduce the ways of thinking of any other type of mind. Why, then, should a particular type of mind or a certain degree of evolution be required in order to beget the typical productions of a certain stage of civilization?

Although the more sober kind of modern historicism tries to avoid cut-and-dried schemes of cycles and recurrences, it does not avoid Vico's basic mistake. If the mind of man changes, and these changes account for the differences between one event and another, between one historical 'period' and another, how is it possible for the historian to understand, nay to know any human fact or action of the past if his mind is different, is a changed mind? When I know by direct experience, say, the typical productions of the baroque, does my mind become baroque? If such is the case there is no evolution, or historical development of the mind. At any one moment the mind can think in the same way as at any other moment. And yet, with a blatant contradiction, historicism presupposes that man has no choice in his decisions. When his mind is of a certain type he cannot but produce certain manifestations of civilization.

Historicism indeed destroys morals because it implies that man is never free. He can act only in conformity with the peculiar bent of his mind, and this bent is due to the historical epoch in which he lives. Yet, by stating that history is the only real science, the historicist implies that he can know the innermost springs of human actions of any epoch. Vico disputed the claims of the natural sciences by denying that man can ever know natural facts as God, their immediate cause, knows them. Yet he stated that historical events are knowable because they are due to human minds, although the intent of another human being is concealed from us as the intentions of God are concealed!

His own religion should have taught Vico that only the Father can see into the secrets of a human soul. Vico's followers, however, instead of turning back to a sensibly moderate appreciation of man's powers, went further, and promised to man, as the serpent promised to Eve, that he would become God by eating the fruit of historical lore. By eliminating any religious consideration, by extolling mankind in its everlasting progress as the true living God, they lost sight of Vico's fundamental argument on behalf of history against science—that we

B

cannot know nature because there is something (God's activity) beyond our knowledge.

There would therefore be no reason to deny to science, as Vico did, a right to perfect knowledge. And indeed, at the latest stage of historicism, we find Croce redeeming science and saying that natural science 'does not contradict or oppose . . . the theory that all real knowledge is historical knowledge'. This means that Vico was wrong and that there is no reason to prefer history to science.

Historical positivism denies that a philosophy of history can exist and tries to avoid historical relativism, but by maintaining that history is the perfect knowledge and that it describes ultimate reality, it is responsible for and shares in the actual eclipse of a true philosophical and scientific spirit in European civilization.

The German historian Lorenz, writing towards the end of the 19th century, complained that the term 'history' had lost any clear significance and that people were expecting from history truths and results which could be gained only in quite different fields of research. Nietzsche himself, after having inquired into the damaging effects of history upon human life, concluded:

In this way men have been discouraged from any deep research into philosophical problems which do not change, and instead of them one goes in for nice investigations of a historical character—what this and that philosopher really thought, whether this or that writing was really due to him. . . .

In the case of religion it is sufficient to point to the example of Troeltsch, the great theologian, a historicist who tried to interpret theology on a historical basis, and whose last works are dedicated to desperate efforts to unwind the tangled skein of historicism so as to be able once again to recognize and to face the timelessness and the absoluteness of God. Worse still is the effect which historicism has had on morals and social life, so apparent in countries (Italy, Germany, Russia) where historicism of one kind or another has become the official creed of the learned. By making even truth and falsehood, right and wrong, good and evil, relative to the passing moods of man in a certain moment of history, historicism undermines faith, love of truth, honesty. It fosters the moral decay of mankind.

It has become a social duty to challenge historicism. As it maintains that history is ultimate reality, that the historian describes absolute truth, we must ask whether history is real, whether the historian tells what in fact happened or whether he spins history out of his own brain and heart. In a word: we must see if the sober, honest conception of history, which was generally accepted before Vico, was not perhaps a sounder conception. This means asking whether history really happened.

Historicism claims that history, while being a production of the historian, is also real. The historicist denies that there is anything beyond historical events. They are the outward expression of a certain stage of the human mind. A certain type of human mind is what it is only because it lives in and through these events. In order to know and to describe past events the historian must live them over again in his own mind. In this way he transforms the past into the present, and past events become contemporary events. Historicism thus maintains that history (meaning history re-lived, history told) is a production of the historian, but denies that history (meaning past events) may have happened otherwise than the historian thinks.

Only when past facts, past acts of men are considered by the historian, do they become historical events—

> Either our history shall, with full mouth,
> Speak freely of our acts, or else our grave,
> Like Turkish mute, shall have a tongueless mouth.

Yet though the facts quoted by the historian are not

'invented' as, for instance, incidents recounted by the novelist, they cannot claim absolute reality. A *fact* (as it may happen in the immediate experience of anybody who perceives it) and an *event* (as it appears to the mind of the historian who reconstructs it on the basis of documentary evidence) are two quite different things. To prove this we must analyse briefly what is meant by 'hard facts'.

What is a real fact? According to some philosophical theories (for instance, the radical empiricism of Mach and the neo-realism of Whitehead) it is inexact even to define it as something 'known' by direct sensation. A fact as perceived by us may be considered both as something in itself and as an occurrence in our mind. Therefore the real fact is neither objective nor subjective, neither external reality nor a thought, idea, or sensation of it. The distinction between thinking and being does not exist in immediate reality. It results only from an artificial classification of facts into mental and non-mental—a classification due to the peculiar requirements of human activity and research.

Yet let us accept as valid the usual distinction between facts as realities in themselves, and our knowledge of them, and apply the term 'fact' to perceived realities only, using the special qualification '*external* facts' for the objects of actual perception and knowledge. In this restricted sense the existence of facts, and of a real 'world' as their aggregate, has a definite meaning, not only if one assumes the external world to be real, but even in phenomenalistic philosophies such as that of Kant. Kant maintained that sensation is not a passive reception of external facts but an act by which our mind creates them (i.e. sensations or intuitions) by 'synthesizing' or giving (by its own receptive activity) a temporal and spatial quality to something which exists independently of our mind but which cannot be perceived in itself. Out of these intuitions the mind builds concepts, and by this conceptual activity it unifies the whole of our experience into an 'objective' reality. A fact is 'real' in so far as it can become an element of the world of our experience which is ordered and ruled by the activity of our reason.

Both a thoroughgoing realist, such as Whitehead, and the Kantian phenomenalist attribute a distinct reality to some of our sensory experiences, as contrasted with fanciful illusions. The idealist too must grant to perceived facts some sort of reality even if he thinks them created by the mind out of nothing, since even the idealist maintains that sensations and experience are the basic elements out of which other forms of thought are built.

We can therefore attribute a distinct, universally acceptable meaning to the term 'fact' in the sense of a real occurrence or 'hard fact', as distinct from something illusory or non-existent.

Now, external facts in their actual reality, as they are immediately perceived, are not the facts considered and studied by the scientist. Philosophy does investigate their reality and tries to elicit their intimate nature. Science on the contrary disregards the reality of the fact as such and reduces it (by abstraction) to something which is no longer 'real'. By this procedure only can the scientist build up a coherent body of knowledge to account for facts, and to act on them in such a way as to obtain practical results.

For instance, a green colour is a real fact, and as such it is something different from both a blue and a yellow colour. If science used real facts as they are, it could never 'explain' the difference between green, yellow and blue. They are three different things, and there is no way of connecting them save by depriving them of their ultimate reality and by considering all of them only as nondescript colour. Only then will it be possible to explain their difference as due to different frequencies of light-waves. Are light-waves more real than the actual

facts, i.e. the several colours? They are not, if by 'real'
fact we mean something perceived. To prove whether
there is really a light-wave this has to be made mani-
fest as a certain colour which can be perceived, or by
some other expedient by which a light-wave produces
something immediately real, i.e. another perceived
fact.

Eddington maintained indeed that science does not
start from facts as they are but from measurements, from
figures read on a scale. Warmth for science is only a
certain reading of the thermometer, colour is only a
certain position on the spectrum, different weights of
bodies are certain readings on a weighing machine. The
so-called 'hard facts' of science are figures, first and last.
Nothing else can be considered by the scientist.

Only when he applies his results, does he transform
his abstract figures and equations and formulas back
to real facts. For instance, when the student of ballistics
teaches the best way of killing somebody, he does not
consider the colour and the general aspect and the many
particulars of your gun—he considers only its power, and
directs you to point it in a certain direction and at a
certain angle if you wish to get a bullet through the head
of your neighbour. A bullet is something more—far
more—than a hitting device. It has colour besides weight;
it is made of a certain material: but to bring about the
desired real fact (the death of your neighbour) you can
disregard everything else but the weight and form in
that 'real fact' which is a bullet. A bullet as a perceived
reality is a bundle of disparate sensations, or a sensation
with manifold aspects. Using it scientifically or practically you can safely disregard its manifold reality and consider in the abstract only those elements or aspects of it
which make of it a good hitting device.

To maintain the paramount worth of history the historicist has, before all else, to prove that he knows and
understands more than the scientist. He therefore libels

science as an abstract activity which disregards reality. Science, he says, achieves results, but does not know anything about real facts. Science is an abstract construction. History alone knows and explains facts, such as they are. The scientist considers arbitrarily isolated aspects of them only, and connects them according to their similarity. But each fact is *that* fact and nothing else. Every fact is absolutely different from every other. Science disregards this difference and considers, for instance, two bullets which have the same weight and dimensions as being absolutely identical, although two bullets are in reality two *different* bullets.

This criticism brought Rickert and other philosophers to investigate the essential difference between the attitude of the scientist and that of the historian. The scientist, they concluded, tends to eliminate differences so as to be able to fit a certain class of facts into a general law—the scientific method aims at establishing laws, is *nomothetic*. The historian tends to distinguish between facts of a similar kind so as to be able to give them a separate identity—history is *idiothetic* or individualizing. And indeed each single battle must be considered as absolutely different from any other; the death of someone as different from any other death, if you have to assign to each fact a determined place in time, and to consider facts as constituting a succession, a temporal sequence. From a scientific point of view any fact can occur again and again. Indeed no experimenting would be possible unless one could try again and again, at any moment, to see if many experiments give the same result. The historicist contends that in this way the scientist forgets that any fact, any thing, any reality is just that thing and nothing else. A fact is unrepeatable—when once it has happened, it will never happen again.

Does the historian himself consider real facts? Do facts, as such, belong to history? In short: is a historical event a real fact? Is it at least more real than the abstract conception considered by the scientist?

Any fact is real in so far as it is that individual one, but in order to become aware of it it is necessary to recognize it. Take for example a burning match. We are aware of it as a certain fact because we compare it with burning matches already seen, and find between them a general similarity. Did we not compare and judge them, we would perceive the fact, but perceiving it does not mean being fully aware of it, having a full cognition of it—in short, *knowing* it. In other words: any sensation is that sensation, any experience is that experience and not another—but we are absolutely incapable of thinking it and of saying anything about it till we have judged it on the basis of the experience of other facts, and recognized it (to take this example) as a burning match, or the picture of a burning match, or a stick of wood, or something else.

The real fact as such, in its essential difference from any other, is beyond our knowing—and indeed only from a philosophical point of view can one assert that facts are fundamental realities. As soon as one is aware of it, it has already been superseded by general conceptions. Sensation does not remain sensation—sensation is blind, is not the sensation 'of something'. In order to be the sensation 'of a certain fact' it must be confronted and compared and judged and recognized.

Now when the historian claims a fact as a historical event, he does not consider it as it is, in its factual individuality, as it would be perceived before being known. He makes of it an individual event only *after* having known it. And since a fact to be known must be compared and judged in relation to other similar ones, the historian, in order to get his strictly individualized event, must disregard just those similarities, those general points of view which have allowed him to know and recognize a fact for what it was. His *idiothetic*, individualizing activity does not bring back the reality of the individual fact as perceived. The historian is confronted with a new, different individual being which results from an abstraction, i.e. from a disregarding and discarding of the similarities between this single fact and others of the same kind.

The fact immediately known to the historian is the same as that immediately known to the scientist. Whilst the scientist discards anything that makes it different from any other of the same kind, the historian discards anything which makes it similar to any other. If the 'fact' of the scientist is an abstraction because it is considered only in so far as it is comparable to other facts, the historical event is no less abstract. The individualizing procedure of the historian does not attain the basic reality of the fact in itself. If the historian considered only the fact in its immediate reality, as sensation apprehends it, he would not *know* his 'events'. He would have only a blind sensation of nondescript facts.

The death of Caesar is a fact totally different from the death, say, of Everyman. It is true that to the eyes of the physiologist they are only two deaths, an abstract conception—in a sense, they are the death of nobody. The historian, however, in concentrating on the one being Caesar's and the other Everyman's, does not consider that he can speak of 'death' only because there are similarities between the death of Caesar and the death of Everyman.

It could still be maintained that reality can only be known by some process of abstraction, and therefore that the lore of the historian is at least as scientific as the knowledge of the scientist. History would still be a science, a positive knowledge, not a fictional creation such as art.

There are however other limits to the knowledge of the historian. The scientist attempts to establish a law, and his aim obliges him to assume that all facts of a kind can be explained in the same way, and in general that any and every one permits of some scientific explanation which will be basically in accord with the scientific explanation of all others. On the other hand, the individualizing point of view of the historian debars him from considering all possible facts. It is indeed impossible for a human mind to consider an infinite number of individual facts. Only a restricted number of them can be thought of and considered. Therefore historical events are abstractions from some facts and not from all of them —not even from the whole of a certain group as they may appear successively to our own or to others' experience. Historical events are abstractions of selected facts.

Is such selection due to the nature and quality of the facts themselves, or to a deliberate and arbitrary act of the historian, such that two historians may choose two quite different sets from the same period and yet claim the same right to consider them as historical events?

All facts have the same reality—the death of Mussolini is no more 'real' than the death of my barber. But the historian will take into account the death of Mussolini and forget the death of my barber, as if they had a different degree of reality. The historian cannot say indeed that my barber was not as real as Mussolini, yet he thinks it legitimate in writing his history to take account of Mussolini's death but not my barber's. This is by itself sufficient to prove that history does not deal with reality as such. Moreover, the historian's choice is not ruled by absolute principles, such that different historians or the same historian are bound always to consider certain facts as historical and others as not, and to draw a fixed line between the historical and the non-historical. Consider some border-line case—for instance the embassy of Edward Herbert in France at the beginning of the Thirty Years' War. If the historian wishes to write British or European history in a very detailed way, he is bound to quote the name of Herbert and to consider his embassy as a historical event. If he writes only a summarized history there is no need to speak of Herbert, of his dealings and of their influence on the Thirty Years' War. Herbert will have descended to the non-historical position of, say, his lackeys only because the historian has altered the frame of his history, and not in consequence of something connected with Herbert as a real being.

To the historian of literature Shakespeare's creation of *Hamlet*, to the historian of science the discovery of blood circulation, to the historian of politics the battle of Bosworth, are events. The historian of politics can pass over Harvey's discovery whilst neither *Hamlet* nor Bosworth need be quoted in a history of science.

It can be answered that true history is general history —the universal history of all the activities of mankind. But even if it were possible to connect and blend into a coherent whole a complex history of literature and science and politics and music and economics, etc., some events would automatically be left out owing to the limited extent of any human knowledge and capability—and therefore they would lose their quality of events.

The historian can answer that he leaves out the 'less important' events which may appear only in a more restricted and specialized history, but this would mean that there are different degrees of 'historical reality'— and thus 'historical reality' does not mean anything, because any thing is either real or not real. There is no middle way. There are no 'degrees' of reality.

The historicist on the contrary maintains that any fact whether quoted or not by the historian does, of its own nature, have a place in history. But either 'historical fact' means something definite, different from other facts, or it does not.

In the first case, the statement '*All* facts are historical' is a contradiction in terms. In the second case, if real fact and 'historical fact' or event are in themselves identical, and reality as such is historical, history cannot be considered as supreme knowledge. *Any* knowledge would be in itself historical, science as well as art, living as well as thinking. It could not then be maintained that history gives a better insight into reality, that history is the highest science, if any kind of knowledge is historical.

The identification of fact and event is impossible. We must admit of some difference between a run-of-the-mill fact and a historical event. Consequently we may ask whether the historian's choice of some facts in the field of our experience which may or must be considered as events, is based on some reasonable criterion.

The facts chosen must fall into an understandable pattern, must be such as to enter into a consistent reasonable narrative. This does not mean that history gives the causal connection between all the historical facts quoted. Historians often deny that their science is bound, as science (broadly speaking) is, to the principle of causality. According to the philosophy of history one fact is not due to another fact: both are due immediately to an underlying reality and their connection results from their belonging to the same pattern of development. Yet any kind of historicism also denies that one event may be caused by another, because causation cannot apply to spiritual events (to human decisions) but to physical facts only.

Still, even if they are not connected by a cause-effect relation, events belong to a coherent pattern, and between events and their pattern there is an intimate correlation. Given a certain pattern, one must take account of certain events. To take other events into account would alter the pattern. This is a rule to which the historian's choice of his events, from amongst nondescript facts, is subjected: events must accord with the pattern, and the pattern is determined by the choice of events. This is immediately evident. Were events real, the pattern likewise would be real and history a description of reality; as it has been proved that events are not real facts, even their pattern does not coincide with the texture of ultimate reality, and is therefore no more 'real' than are events themselves. In other words: an event has a meaning only in regard to the general pattern of history. Therefore the choice of events determines their meaning, and the meaning (i.e. pattern) which the historian thinks they have, determines the choice.

The internal coherence of chosen events, selected pattern and intended meaning is related to the reality of empirical facts by one circumstance alone—that events are abstracted from real facts. Therefore documentary research, checking of data, etc. are necessities in the work of the historian. This is the only 'scientific' aspect of the craft of history. And indeed in 'establishing his facts' the historian has to follow the general methods and rules established by the scientist to make sure of the reality of his data.

It must, however, be emphasized that the whole of earthly occurrences, even if these could all be elicited and collected, would not be history. There would be no historical pattern, since such a pattern depends upon choice and connects individual abstractions. The general pattern of all real facts is the very nature of reality in and by itself. And it is for the philosopher to know and to describe it.

The overall form assumed by a historical pattern is that of a temporal sequence. This might seem to prove that history and reality are interrelated since it does appear incontrovertibly true that any fact happens either before or after another fact. Only in consequence of an act of abstraction can a scientific datum occur again and again, be (theoretically) experienced and checked without considering the time-sequence to which it belongs. An event on the other hand must be placed in time just because it is unique. A single, isolated occurrence, different from any other occurrence, can only 'happen' once, in a certain moment. An event is such a one and not another both because *idiothetic* abstraction gives it a peculiar character and because it happens at a certain moment. Individual characteristics and temporal individualization are inter-related. It has been proved that individualization is the result of a process of abstraction. It must now be proved that the time-sequence in which each historical event has a fixed place has no absolute reality and is a fictitious structure which has been formed in consequence of the peculiar needs of history as an abstract construction.

Time, according to St. Augustine, is only an 'extension' of the soul. Past and future do not really exist. Only the flying present, the instantaneous 'now', exists. We live, we *are*, in the passing moment only, and from it we proceed to another moment and then to another, till death stops the continuous change which is human life. Our world is as changeable and impermanent as we. God on the contrary lives in a permanent moment because, being perfect and infinite, He cannot change, or pass over from one moment to another. God's eternity is *tota simul*, all contemporaneous. To our time-experience, God's eternal present may appear as an infinite succession of moments or as a single everlasting present—but in fact it is neither a succession nor a present moment. It is a temporal situation completely different from the kind of time in which we live. Were it asked what God did before creating the world, one should answer that before the world was created time did not exist, and therefore there was no 'before'.

St. Augustine's distinction between eternity and time shows that when one asks about the reality of time in general, one does not take account of the fact that there are or may be different *kinds* of time. Even the time in which we live and in which the world exists assumes different shapes according to our consideration. Scientific time differs substantially from the time of which, by the succession of our moods and feelings, we have direct experience. This 'psychic' time cannot be measured:

one can say that a certain feeling or sensation comes before another, but there is no means by which to judge whether the interval between two states of one's mind is longer or shorter than that between two others. Our psychic life simply flows (as Bergson says) from past to future in a continuous stream. It is not possible to contemplate this flow from an external, fixed point so as to be able to measure its flowing. External happenings on the contrary have a measurable velocity (which is space and time blended together) because they happen in space no less than in time. The scientist is able to tell the length of a certain stretch of time.

History happens in yet another kind of time. Psychic past and present and future are *qualitatively* different: our present consciousness is a clear-cut dividing line between the past and the future which are both real (or unreal) in the same way, in our memory and in our expectation. The historian too accepts the distinction, but for him the past is perfectly real; the future, simply, does not exist. A historical event is essentially a past event as distinct from any present and future occurrence. The historian could never invert the temporal succession —an event comes either before or after another event. In scientific time, on the contrary, 'past' and 'present', 'before' and 'after' are relative. By measuring data in a certain way two facts are successive; by measuring them in another way they are contemporary.

There is no reason to assume that one of these three kinds of time is time in the absolute, 'real' time. Anyway, historical time could never claim such a privileged position, because it involves an inconsistency.

An event indeed is an event only when and because it is past. On the other hand, if history were a knowledge of something which really happened, the historian should be able to experience again, to know, to live the past event just as it happened, i.e. to transform it from a past into a present event. It was indeed noted above that the historicist is bound to aver that all history is contemporary history. This strange conception is maintained outspokenly by celebrated historicists—by Croce, by Gentile and by many others. Yet the very essence of a historical event is that it happened and (in consequence of its *idiothetic* individualization) that it could not possibly happen again. If the event as it happened and the event as thought of afterwards by the historian are absolutely the same event, everything can happen again and again, there is no distinction between past and present—there are no historical events at all, nor any history. To escape this consequence one must assume that the event as made present again, as re-lived by the historian, is more or less different from the same event as it occurred. And this means again that the historian does not deal with facts as they really happened.

The historicist's conception implies a further absurdity as to historical time. If history is absolutely real it is infinite, endless. On the other hand history is always referred to man, to human events, to events as known by the historian who is a man. Therefore the endless development of human reality makes mankind climb higher and higher towards infinite perfection. God (this was the basic assumption of Comte and Feuerbach and Hegel) is only mankind in its infinite progress.

If it be assumed that history never ends it must also be assumed that history never began. One must be able to trace history backwards, to lower and lower forms of humanity and life, and finally to mindless, material being. But is not inanimate being the object of natural science? It would then seem that science, instead of being the opposite of history as the historicist maintains, is already history when the latter is assumed as stretching endlessly in the past.

Therefore, in retracing the past (i.e. thinking and writing history) the historian must stop somewhere, at the point where history ceases to be such because there is no mankind for whom it could happen. Even Hegel himself, the holy father of historicism, was unable to give any good reason why history should begin somewhere. He wrote indeed: 'It is only proper and dignified for philosophical consideration to assume that history began when rationality appeared in the world.' But then it should be no less 'proper and dignified' for history to end somewhere in the future, to deny endless progress, to allow for the existence of God beyond history. This would mean taking up again the old, sound idea that history begins at a certain point (the Creation) and ends with the Last Judgment.

By making history paramount, the historicist puts himself in a quandary. Either history begins and ends (and then it is not paramount), or it never begins and never ends, and then it is not history throughout. Vico understood this quandary obscurely, and to escape it he postulated that history goes on endlessly *but* by successive phases each one of which has a beginning and an end. History runs neither in a closed circle nor along an infinite straight line: it goes spiralling forwards endlessly. In this way Vico was able to believe in a God beyond history. History advances in a certain direction, but it ends and must begin again and again because of the finiteness of man as against the eternity of God.

Vico's conception was of course wilful and irrational, chiefly because the condition of man between the end of one civilization and the beginning of another was not clear. Is the true barbarian a rational being?—then he must have some kind of civilization. Is he not?—then whence comes the mind which will create the next civilization? Spengler tried to make this construction reasonable by affirming that there is no God but an obscure destiny (*Schicksal*) which keeps mankind tied to recurring cycles, and that what recur are not historical events as such but only their general form. He main-

C

tained that in any historical event there is a substance
and a form: Cromwell and his actions as a dictator as
against the general historical *form* of dictatorship. No
other Cromwell is possible, but many and many dictator-
ships of the same kind have happened in the past and
will happen in the future.

The distinction between matter and form of a historical event is an arbitrary assumption. Why should one
consider only dictatorship as the general form of that
complex, many-sided event which was the career of
Cromwell? Why should one not consider the general
form of this career as an example of strategic capacity, or
of a religious mind, and give Cromwell a meaning as
belonging to military history, or to the history of religion,
rather than to the history of politics?

On the other hand if one accepts the distinction between
the matter and the form of historical events, and considers philosophy of history as the science of historical
forms, history would posit laws, and would no longer
individualize events. History then would become anthropology, a natural science. How could morphology of
history, a science of permanent laws, be blended with
history as an account of individual events, one different
from another?

It is evident that any cycle-theory of history, be it
Vico's or Spengler's, is unsound. It affords no escape
from the basic difficulty, that history must be considered,
at one and the same time, both as having a beginning and
end, and as happening in unlimited time. Historical time
is not real time, true time. It is only one of the possible
conceptions of time, less rational and 'real' because it is
inconsistent in itself. It is at the same time both endless
and limited. Historical past and historical present are
different, and yet identical. Historical time is indeed only
a special frame which the historian must use in order to
weave on it his charming tissue of 'all our yesterdays'—
a tale full of sound and fury which comes to signify some-

thing only owing to the creative power of the historian.

It might be objected that if historical events have a place only in an abstract, arbitrary time, they are at any rate individualized by reason of their happening in a certain place. Chronology and geography are indeed the eyes of history. Geography seems to describe exactly the place of an event, so that even if the point in time in which something happened is unreal, yet the point in space is real.

Geography, however, is another abstraction. One can check on a map the position, say, of the battle of Waterloo —but the battle of Waterloo was not fought on a map but in a landscape. The map reproduces only some elements of a landscape, and those only by allusion, by special conventions—blue for water, green for a forest, etc. The landscape (colours, geological peculiarities, weather, etc.) does not contribute to the individualization of the battle of Waterloo. Some elements of the real landscape in which the battle happened may enter into a rational description of the battle—the weather, the hills, etc.—but it is quite useless, indeed impossible to pretend to describe it as taking place where it was actually fought. The real place consisted of a number of elements which did not influence the course of the battle. Nevertheless the mere geographical (abstract) connotation of the place by so many degrees of latitude and longitude, taken together with the temporal connotation (and time and space are not interchangeable in history as they are in the case of scientific calculation), is perfectly sufficient to make of that battle an individual occurrence, i.e. an abstract historical event.

History did not happen, yet the historian makes it happen—for his reader. History is created by the craft of the historian. The best way to describe this craft is to compare it with such other productions of the human brain as science and fiction. In comparison with the latter, the facts from which historical events are elicited are 'real' occurrences—the historian does not create his events out of nothing, but abstracts them from reality as known by his or others' experience. In comparison with science the basic pattern of history is temporal. Events can be expounded coherently only when they are described as following the course of abstract historical time.

We have already seen that the scientist (any kind of scientist) does not deal with real (experienced and experimental) facts but with an abstraction which makes scientific data of them. He too must fit his data into a coherent pattern, but the pattern of science is not principally temporal, and the goal of science is to find laws, not to describe individuals.

These points of difference between history and other human productions and activities are formal distinctions. We have deliberately avoided till now any consideration of the subject-matter of history. To complete our description of history we must now examine it. Historical abstraction always works upon facts in so far as they are human or related to mankind, whilst the biologist's data are relative to life in general, or the chemist's data imply differences of elements.

The so-called 'social sciences' (sociology, anthropology, jurisprudence, economy, etc.) also deal with human elements and human events, but they do not consider men as individuals. The sociologist could, so to speak, 'exchange' any individual man for another. The historian, even when he speaks of mass-movements, of the 'spirit of the age', must always be able to take account of single individuals or of the particular acts of somebody. History therefore is not a science. As it cannot point out laws, it describes each occurrence as something apart, and refers every event to the action or to the existence of non-interchangeable individuals.

This reference to men as individuals can be made only by man, and by a certain man. An electronic brain may do the work of the mathematician, or a camera the work of a scientific observer, but only a man can recognize and collect and abstract facts into historical events.

The innermost essence of an event is its reference to an individual. Even when denying free will, and attributing human actions to economic or other non-human causes, history still considers these causes as acting through human beings as their instruments. The human quality of the historian and of his subject, interrelated as they are, makes us turn with a deeper appreciation to the ancient conception of history as a form of art.

The scientist is human, but his subject-matter is not. Only his brain is involved—the rest of him, feelings and inherited tendencies and sexual complexes and physiological peculiarities and his free volition may have influenced his choice of a certain science as his subject, but generally speaking his individual peculiarities are assumed not to have influenced his results. On the contrary, the artist is deeply involved in his artistic creation. He is not just a brain. Any individual peculiarity of his may be reflected in his work. And one can always trace in any work of art some elements which are due to the human qualities of the artist—even to his physiological peculiarities. Criticism would otherwise be impossible. There would be no motivation for that strongly individual character, that absolute uniqueness which is the first, most arresting aspect of any artistic creation.

The historian's attention too, is drawn to certain aspects of a fact (or to certain facts) by his individual peculiarities. Be these conscious or instinctive, natural or due to reflective thinking, his choice is *his* own choice and nobody else's. The pattern of his history is influenced by his whole human personality.

Although one historian may choose the very same historical occurrences as another, quite a different history will result from his efforts at seeing them in their particulars.

Think for a moment what might have been written by Tacitus, the die-hard republican, had he tried to write the history of a more ancient period of Roman history, as Livy, the idealist admirer of divine Rome, had done. What might result from Professor Trevelyan's re-writing of Xenophon's *Anabasis*, or Professor Toynbee's re-writing of Gibbon's *Decline and Fall?*

Of course the paramount motivation of the historian is due to his conscious feelings and leanings and beliefs. He sees happenings from the standpoint of his political (or other) leanings and comes easily to the conclusion that history teaches what he would like to have everybody thinking and doing. *Historia magistra vitae*—yes, indeed, but because occurrences are looked at by every historian in such a way that only his own conception of life can be used to connect them, to give them a coherent pattern.

*Opus oratorium maxime*, a matter of persuading people, a plea for or against some course of future action. Whilst an attorney can select evidence, can even bribe witnesses and pack juries to get the wished-for coherent pattern, the historian cannot. If he dismisses relevant testimonials, too many ascertained and documented facts (i.e. if he refuses to give to them the quality of events), he fails because his jury is made up of every possible reader who may know (having read many other historians already) the real evidence in the case, and does not like the construction put by the historian on his events.

The great historian is he who takes in the greatest possible number of facts and gives to them a coherent pattern. Sometimes it may happen that, if he is really a good historian, he perceives that the pattern cannot be coherent unless he gives another slant to his events, and then he produces a pattern at variance with his previous opinion. In such a case the historian is in the position of a novelist who starts on a rough draft of his novel, and then is compelled by the development of his characters and of his situations considerably to alter his original scheme.

Here, one might be tempted to think that the pattern of history is logical, as that of a mathematical theorem, whilst the scheme of a novel is not bound to logical rules. This is not true. In a theorem no human element is considered and therefore no free decision can intervene to alter the results. Yet even the unforeseen decisions of a character must accord with his human peculiarities—and anyway the very mutability of human decisions imposes on the novelist the logical need to take into account even the possible variations of his characters. From a certain standpoint any narrative (both fictional and historical) is bound to logic no less than an exposition of Einstein's theory. But whilst the novelist can freely invent and change the actions of his characters, the historian cannot because these actions are past, already fixed.

The artistic difference between history and fiction may be elicited from a cursory examination of the historical novel. In it historical and fictional facts are combined together—but the pattern is historical and there are limits to the allowable invention of the novelist. He is bound not only by the internal logic of his characters but even by the logical coherence of the historical pattern. Therefore Manzoni, a historical novelist himself, was right when he averred that the historical novel is inconsistent as a literary *genre*. Certainly it is apt to become either a dreary tale (by a too exact adherence to historical events and pattern), or too fanciful, and then the historical pattern breaks up and the novel lacks the impressive appearance of reality to which it owes its attraction.

Any historical novelist has to put together historical occurrences which are fixed because they have already happened, and inventions which (being undetermined) are rather occurrences in the future than past events.

Invention and documentary evidence are mixed. The
reader feels always a sort of shiftiness. When there are
no documented facts, the novelist invents them. If a
better, more accurate documentation were on hand, he
could not invent. It is as if one took advantage of the
unavoidable blanks of historical evidence—an unfair
advantage. A historical novel appears indeed as a provisional work, to be accepted till better information be
available.

Bound as he is by his peculiar aims and theses and
teachings, by the reality of physical happenings from
which to abstract his historical events, by the duty of
logical coherence, by the fundamental human quality of
his subject-matter—what can the historian do as an
artist? It is quite useless to discuss here the nature and
meaning of art, but any theory of art teaches that the
artist creates. The historian is limited by the conditions
inherent to historical pattern and facts, yet he still enjoys
artistic latitude, and can create something, because he
can choose his words and shape freely the style of his
narration.

A portrait- or landscape-painter does not invent his
subject-matter and its peculiarities. Yet by choosing his
hues, by stressing a line here and a shape there, he soars
above his subject. He is able to conjure up the impalpable
meaning of a landscape, the elusive spirit of a living man.
By being bound and restricted on all sides, his artistic
powers show themselves at their best. His work can
result either in photographic likeness—and then he is no
more an artist than is a camera—or it can result in a
living soul or a landscape seen in their essentials, and as
no one has ever seen them before. Then, only then, is
he an artist.

The historian too can treat, so to speak, of certain things
only, but he is free to choose the way of conveying them.
His words, his historical periods, the plan of the book are

in his power. In choosing his facts he had to be loyal to his intentions and careful of the internal logicality of his narration. Yet in describing his events, he *creates* reality. History is as real as any other 'real' happening because it is something in and by itself: a work of art.

Artistic skill alone can give the reader the sense of historical nemesis which can be conveyed by a thorough-going coherence of historical narration. The historian's way of presenting the course of happenings will make of them either events which fit easily into the pattern of history and into his peculiar conception of the world, or else stillborn abstractions, facts which have lost reality without gaining the immortal life of art. Chronicles, year-books, chronology, the newspapers also give facts— facts which tomorrow will be historical events only if a historian arises who is able to give them unity, such compactness that the reader will have the feeling that no occurrence has been overlooked, no relevant element passed over. The historian who invents, or does not check his evidence sufficiently or forgets too many facts is not simply a dishonest historian. He is not only an inefficient pleader. He is also a bad artist.

The historian cannot leave out facts at will for the sake of unity. The clash between *his* narration, and what the reader knows already of the events described by the historian would destroy the persuasive force of his work. This should be as compelling as the persuasive force which makes of a great painting, of a great symphony something one can never escape after having once seen or heard it. It remains—a block, a monument in one's memory and mind, an element of one's innermost self. You will never be able to think about an epoch of man-kind, about a nation, about an aspect of civilization but as the great historian has presented them. You will never escape his history. Your own life appears a prosecution of it. Life seems to have meaning and depth only when you think yourself into that historical pattern.

True history is conclusive, as if the period described, the set of events chosen were really, as every human thing is, closed up and concluded, between a beginning and an end, in a perfect unbreakable circle. Then, and then only, is history—any history—a perfect counterpart of the whole history of mankind. The historian re-echoes, under a partial aspect, with a subdued tone, the immense rhythmic clause of universal history from its opening note to its triumphant finale:

And the Angel which I saw stand upon the sea and upon the earth, lifted up his hand to heaven,

And sware by Him that liveth for ever and ever, who created heaven and the things that therein are, and the sea, and the things that are therein, that there should be time no longer . . . —ὅτι χρόνος οὐκέτι ἔσται.

CHAPTER II

# HISTORY OF PHILOSOPHY—
# HISTORY OR LEGEND?

> ... ne pecorum ritu sequamur
> antecedentium gregem.
>
> SENECA

L ET US state clearly and uncompromisingly that philosophy is the highest study of which human reason,
in and by itself, is capable. Yet the keen edge of
philosophical enquiry has always been blunted by historical prejudice, by the assumption that any philosopher
must fall into line with his predecessors and find his place
in the so-called 'history of philosophy'.

This limits the scope of original research, and gives to
it an initial slant. The thinker is caught in the troublesome 'circle' of philosophy and history of philosophy.
How can one know what philosophy is without having
read other philosophers or learnt history of philosophy?
And how can one understand philosophers and history of
philosophy without already knowing what philosophy is?

Elaborate paths out of this maze have been designed
by many philosophers—idealists especially, and first
amongst them Gentile. Perhaps there is a short cut
—'history of philosophy', simply, does not exist. It is
only a myth invented by timid thinkers afraid to embark
alone 'in the intense inane', towards final truth. The
herd-instinct is too strong even in minds given to pure
speculation.

History of philosophy can be detailed as a sequence of
self-contained monographs, or described as a continuous
trend of philosophical thought running from one to
another thinker—a distinction which roughly corresponds to that between historical positivism and philosophy
of history.

The first kind, written usually by people with no strong
systematic interests or a personal philosophy of their own,
is a succession of isolated accounts of the thought of each
philosopher of note, and of his opinions on the great
philosophical questions. All philosophers are considered

as it were on the same level, side by side, without any
attempt at establishing a hierarchy of better and worse
systems of philosophy, or a general trend of philosophical
thought. An early example of this kind of history is that
of Diogenes Laertius who dealt in each chapter or book
with a single philosopher, or philosophers of the same
'school' connected actually as pupil to teacher, or as
champions of the same kind of conception. It was a
'doxography', that is, a description of opinions. Plutarch, instead, had given to his doxography the form of a repertory,
ordered according to the several philosophical problems
or concepts—say, 'world', 'soul', etc.—and listing under
each head the different conceptions of philosophers on
the world, the soul, etc.

On the other hand, history of philosophy as a continuous development, as 'philosophy of the history of philosophy', may claim Aristotle himself as its ancestor since he
supported his conceptions by an exposition of his predecessor's theories of being, and tried to show that there
had been a gradual improvement of philosophical thought
and that it had culminated in his own metaphysics.

Even after twenty centuries or so, the two types of
history of philosophy are easily recognizable: doxographies, such as the histories by Hoffding, Windelband,
Eucken, and more recently Russell and Copleston; and
'philosophies of history' such as Hegel's *Vorlesungen* and
a number of others. Many philosophers indeed are tempted to prove that their philosophy is the final result, the
perfect, ripe fruit of a long line of outstanding thinkers.

We must deal severally with the conception of 'history
of philosophy' according to doxographers and according to
the 'philosophers of history of philosophy'.

Can doxographies be considered as histories? To present a succession of thinkers in this way may be entertain-
ing or interesting, but what does it really mean? What
can it possibly *teach* concerning philosophy?

There is indeed no reasonable ground for choosing one philosopher rather than another for inclusion in a disconnected history of philosophy of this sort. If one assumes that 'important' philosophers only are to be considered, one falls again into a historical preconception. A philosopher seems to be important because we arrange cultural history in such a way that his ideas are put into relief. On the other hand if we choose philosophers only because they had many followers, or because they were more widely and more often read by posterity, their success may have been due to accidental reasons—good propaganda on the part of the philosopher and his immediate pupils; their ability in getting teaching jobs; the preservation of certain writings whilst those of other thinkers' have been lost; or simply, ignorance of the complexities of thought, laziness on the part of a posterity that has picked up celebrated names and writings without enquiring about others because these were less known and popular. When indeed a thoroughgoing student tries to deal in earnest with the cultural conditions of a certain epoch and country, he is always able to discover, in some dusty corner of a library, books much more interesting and deeper than those usually quoted as standard documents of the cultural situation of their epoch.

Nobody can maintain that the list of philosophers dealt with in any respectable 'history of philosophy' of this kind, accords with any reasonable rule. The list includes philosophers who maintained contrasting theories on the nature of being and knowing. One finds Parmenides side by side with Heraclitus, Plato with Aristotle, Epicurus with Seneca, Aquinas with Duns Scotus, Bacon with Descartes, Hobbes with Malebranche, Hegel with Herbart, Rosmini with Spencer. Could all of them possibly have been right? To justify this juxtaposition of contraries by saying that doxographies presuppose that truth lies in the middle is to accept the contention of the 'philosopher of history of philosophy', that there is an overall 'history' of philosophy in which all philosophers are connected. This we hope to prove groundless. To quote them one by one because of some vague tradition which makes them seem relevant, is not to be concerned with 'philosophy' at all. It is to compile a sort of Golden Legend. One does not know whether they are important because they were right, or because they were utterly wrong; whether it is a Legend of the Saints or a museum of spiritual monsters.

The argument can be brought a step further. Accept the official list, forget that this sparse 'history of philosophy' can teach little concerning philosophy since by reading one great philosopher one must un-learn the lesson of the preceding chapter, which dealt with a philosopher of quite different views. Let us put on blinkers and forgetting everybody else read the chapter on, say, Schelling. How can one describe 'the philosophy' of Schelling, who more than once radically changed his philosophical allegiance? The case of Schelling is perhaps exceptional. But as a matter of fact the thought of every great philosopher evolved and passed through successive stages. Sometimes the last stage was different from, but consistent with, the first, sometimes it was quite incompatible with it. Plato began by averring the existence of a separate world of ideas, but ended by refuting it. Berkeley and Kant betrayed their own initial theories. What can one describe as 'the philosophy' of Plato, or Berkeley, or Kant? One can choose a certain stage in the development of the thought of each, and expound their philosophy at that stage as a consistent system, but in this case 'Plato', 'Berkeley', 'Kant' are only labels pasted on an abstract figment which has nothing to do with Plato, Berkeley or Kant who as living thinkers did but pass through that stage. In this way one denies they had a right to search further and change their minds, as if these 'great' thinkers should be judged foolish in going on with their research beyond the stage chosen by the doxographer as philosophically relevant.

To avoid such arbitrary slicing of lives dedicated to philosophy, one might describe instead the development of their thought, the source of their specialised attention to certain problems, their late discovery of some imperfection or inconsistency which made them inquire further and change their views. This would be a biography of a thinker, and, as biography, worthwhile. But what of philosophy? From the example of such a life one could learn loyalty to truth and single-minded devotion to research, but not some philosophical truth to be accepted as it stands. The last stage of the thinker was the last because he died, not because he had reached ultimate truth. Death made him stop enquiring and changing his mind.

Let us now turn to the other conception of the history of philosophy—to the assumption of a line of development connecting the several thinkers. These, then, would be in a sense only the mouthpieces of mankind's philosophical thinking in a certain epoch.

If this is true, no philosopher can ever hope to discover any relevant truth. The world will go on, more thinkers will appear, a further stage of development will be reached. History makes a fool of philosophy.

It is easy indeed to disprove this pretence—which amounts simply to a denial of philosophy as such—by quoting again the doubts expressed in the first chapter concerning any kind of philosophy of history. But in the case of philosophy we may appeal to specific criticism. What evidence is available to prove a development of philosophical thought throughout the ages?

It will be claimed in the next chapter that the conception of 'progress', in general, is a myth. In the particular case of philosophy a steady improvement could only be due either to accumulated knowledge or to an improved thinking capacity on the part of later philosophers.

The first alternative has often been proposed, for instance by Brunschvicg in *Les âges de l'intelligence*. It is only the age-honoured mediaeval argument, taken up again by Bacon, that even if individually we are poorer thinkers than were the Greek philosophers, we can use the accumulated discoveries of all previous thought. A pigmy on the shoulders of a giant sees further than the giant himself. Brunschvicg maintains that we must be more intelligent, more knowledgeable than older thinkers were because we are in a position to use knowledge acquired in many former centuries of philosophical research.

This argument does not take into consideration the clear-cut alternatives between different metaphysical conceptions. One cannot be both a realist and an idealist, an empiricist and a rationalist, etc. No thinker can really avail himself of all data accumulated in centuries of research. He can, at the utmost, use only the partial data evolved in a particular philosophical school.

Even within these very restricted limits can we assume that the platonism, say, of latter-day Platonists is better than Plato's own?—A *prima facie* case against this may be made by observing that sometimes a Platonist takes up the philosophy of his immediate predecessors without looking further backwards, yet he could also go back 'to the source', to Plato's text, and start from there, and there is no reason to suppose that he would be worse off.

This is so true that at least twice in the current of European thought philosophy has merged into philology, when thinkers argued about what Plato *had really said* instead of asking whether he, or any of his followers, were right. Renaissance thinkers tried to restate Plato's (and Aristotle's and Plotinus') true meaning and ideas rather than to evolve from him a new philosophy of their own. The same thing happened in the 19th century in Germany. It seemed then worthwhile to re-establish texts, pristine documents in their integrity, not only as a

D

groundwork for the proper understanding of a philosopher, but as if *philological* inquiry into his true meaning
was in itself a *philosophical* research. Such a dreary con-
fusion between the letter and the spirit was possible only
because as a matter of fact no thinker is obliged to go on
from the last stage—he can take the development of any
school at any stage, and start independently from there.

A desperate situation indeed. To save philosophy and
its 'progress' one had to resort to the assumption that it
did not matter what philosophers stated as results of
their research. A progress could be found not in the
results but in the way of setting philosophical problems.
The progress of philosophy would be proved by the
gradual refinement of the questions asked, not of the
answers given. Thought would improve because it asked
harder and harder questions—not because it gave better
answers.

But this 'improvement' is mainly a matter of *transla-
tion*. By translating our problems into the philosophical
'language' and terminology of ancient philosophers, we
find that they were already their problems. Obstinacy in
dealing with a certain set of problems may bring about a
re-shaping of the problem we found insoluble—does it
prove that we are more skilled? Where is the evidence
that our way of asking is deeper and more searching than
older ways?

A way to prove philosophical 'progress', might be to
compare different kinds of philosophy, say, Chinese philosophy as against European thought. But a comparative
examination is impossible. Any non-European philosophy
can be understood by Europeans only on the basis of
their own ways of thinking. The innermost spirit of
other philosophies cannot be elicited from the standpoint
of a different culture. If this were not so, it would mean
that non-European philosophies were only variations of
European philosophy, and then they would not afford a
useful term of comparison. This is evident to everybody

who reads Masson-Oursel's *La philosophie comparée*, a first cautious endeavour in this field.

The presumption of philosophical development rests upon an arbitrary selection and arrangement of some evidence which could equally well be chosen and arranged in many other ways. Even if the historical arrangement seems to demonstrate a progress towards a better understanding of philosophical problems, nobody can tell whether this improvement might be the result only of obstinacy in dealing with intractable problems, i.e. with problems which cannot be solved because they were posited in the wrong way by the 'founders' of philosophical schools.

Evidence shows that no-one has ever started philosophizing on his own. It is not that to know what philosophy is one has to learn history of philosophy. It is strictly a matter of personal training and information. Within any philosophical school, in classical times and at mediaeval and contemporary universities, the pupil sits at the feet of a teacher. A solitary thinker may resort to any classical work of philosophy, of any time.

In either case a thinker is always connected to some other, or more, thinkers. The influence of predecessors works in different ways. As soon as a clever novice knows enough he may try to develop what he has learnt. He comes to see imperfections, insufficient analysis, inconsistencies in his predecessor, and can try to patch up. Very often, out of desperation, he turns against his teachers, he reneges on 'his school', he goes to the opposite side—he becomes a realist after having been apprenticed to an idealist master, an empiricist after a rationalist training.

Different philosophies, the 'schools' of philosophy, 'history' of philosophy are made up just of this interplay of living and dead influences, of present masters and old books, of orthodoxy and heresy. Anything can happen— what can never happen is for any thinker to undertake philosophical research in a way completely independent of, and different from that of one or more of his predecessors. Even when opposing them he is bound to consider the same problems as they considered, to think of the task of a philosopher in the same way as his teachers and his textbooks have considered it.

This is what is really 'historical', meaning inescapable and one-sided, in the sequence of philosophers. 'Starting anew' only means starting from the same starting point, in the same direction, with the same slant. In the immense field of possible research into the ultimate nature and structure of being, nobody ever expatiated at random. The car of philosophy runs on rails. And the starting point was never fixed by philosophical enquiry. It became philosophical by interpretation—originally it was suggested by religion or science or poetry or anything else but philosophy.

If this is true, if the long, intersecting lines of thinkers started always from a peculiar way of looking at reality without sufficient rational grounds for their choice, it is possible to explain why, despite the genius of so many thinkers, a satisfactory solution could never be found. If the initial bias itself was never approached in a critical way, and philosophers just went on from some predecessor without discussing his point of departure, this would explain both why there are always at least two opposite solutions of the same problem—the well-known schizophrenia of philosophy, realist $v.$ idealist, empiricism $v.$ rationalism, and so on—and why schools and systems of philosophy go on and on, every votary of them trying to fill up gaping holes and to gloss over inconsistencies in his own school and system.

One may regard this supposition of a mistaken approach inherited by all thinkers as a far-fetched hypothesis. But let us see whether this hypothesis can explain what is usually described as 'the history of ancient philosophy' and 'the history of modern philosophy'.

If we take a leaf from the book of the historian, we can fix a rough chronology which centres on Plato (428-348 B.C.), the paramount philosopher who exercised so lasting and so deep an influence on European thinkers of every epoch. Plato lived only two centuries after Thales (c. 585 B.C.), the reputed initiator of our 'history of philosophy'. From the viewpoint of the 20th century, Plato ought to be considered a very primitive thinker instead of remaining a living force in our own times. The advance of thought from Thales to Plato must indeed have been exceptionally swift and fruitful if Plato has not, after twenty-three centuries, been ousted, as he in his time ousted Thales.

This is indeed an absurd computation, but it shows the possible results of accepting historical progress at its face-value. There is, in fact, no available evidence to prove peculiarly deep insight on the part of pre-Socratic philosophers. A careful examination of the 'development' of primitive philosophy reveals no sign of genius. Even an average mind could have taken any of the steps that led from Thales to Plato. The pre-Socratics started with a basic bias and never broadened their outlook to include any other approach, nor did they try a new starting point. Thales himself was not the discoverer of anything new. He certainly did not originate European philosophy, for the very good reason that he was no philosopher in the proper sense of the word. Ancient doxographers never referred to him as a discoverer of philosophical truths. For them the term 'philosopher' meant somebody who wanted to know, and to become a wise man; and Thales was considered a *physiologist*, a physicist, who inquired after the nature of *material* being, not of being in general. The 'being' of which he spoke was only the visible world. Even on this limited problem he borrowed his theories, and did not create them.

Before the days of Thales, in the dawn of civilization, some human groups became cultivators, instead of nomadic food-gatherers, on the deltas and the banks of great rivers, the Tigris, the Euphrates and the Nile. Their totemic mentality merged gradually into an animistic conception of natural forces, into hylozoism, the conception of matter as animated by living forces, as living matter.

On the other hand, the great flood or floods which before 2500 B.C. submerged the first seats of Sumerian civilization, near the Persian Gulf, gave rise to the Flood legend, which perhaps was responsible in the Near East for the idea that everything had emerged from water, that God was 'moving upon the face of the waters' at the very beginning of the world. Thales, who belonged to a people with different religious beliefs, 'laicized', as it were, the dogma of water-creation, and by considering it as a rational hypothesis initiated European science. Neither Thales nor his immediate successors seem to have understood that there was another, and truly philosophical, problem to be solved before stating that water or air was the basic stuff—namely the problem whether the reduction of the manifold phenomena to a single underlying matter was a valid explanation. They did not even ask whether the unity of material being was to be established on the basis of a unity of material components of the world, or rather of a unique law regulating the world's multiplicity. They began from the water-hypothesis which they had found ready-made, and which seemed something quite elaborate to people who were unused to scientific speculation.

They asked only: *Why* water? Why not air or fire? And *how*, water? Is water the seed of other elements and of every different quality? Or are all things, of any kind whatsoever, water in disguise? Anaximander understood the difficulty and denied that the basic element, the 'matter' of the universe, could be called 'water' rather than 'air' or 'fire'. It was, he claimed, simply nondescript matter. Another thinker of his school surmised that the process which transforms primeval matter into different 'matters' and things, was only one of rarefaction and condensation. Things were different not because they were made of different 'raw materials' but because they contained more or less matter. Thus Pythagoras was brought to affirm that the world was made of numbers, because by assuming different quantities of the unities of matter, he could explain the difference between, say, air and solid bodies.

These abstract discussions did not have a deep scientific meaning. Pre-Socratic philosophers did not inquire whether the philosophical problem of being could be posited in such restricted terms. They did not use observation and experiment to solve it in a scientific way. Their natural science was still so primitive that they supposed that the sky was a solid vault. Anaximander was the first to advance the hypothesis that the sky was spherical around a flat earth. Moreover, many of them (Xenophanes, Heraclitus, Parmenides) expounded their conceptions in poems which contained rather a fanciful vision of nature than a logically valid explanation of it.

They evaded the problems of *why* and *when* the development of such primeval matter had originated, and where it would end, by supposing it had begun again and again and would begin, again and again, as a succession of recurring world-cycles. This idea too was probably borrowed from Indian or Chaldean speculations.

Early Greek philosophers never came to grips with the downright contradiction involved in the assumption of a *single* principle or matter as the origin or 'root' of *many* different objects. Instead of questioning the soundness of the assumption they asked what could properly be called 'real' and 'existent': the changing shapes and bodies we see around us, or the unique primeval matter of which they are made. Some—the Eleatic sect—maintained that there was one matter only, in a spherical form, and that everything else was illusion. Some, like Heraclitus, said that being was in itself change, but at the same time supposed that everything was made of fire, the most mutable element. Evidently they were unable as yet to distinguish between immobility in space, and permanence of form, between change as a process, and a changing matter.

It was on the basis of such inchoate conceptions that pre-Socratics came to posit a difference between thinking and being, and to dismiss the hylozoistic idea that matter was in itself a living and thinking being. No peculiar genius was needed in order to reach the conclusion that, if change is illusory, and we are yet able to know that it is an illusion and to posit the unity and immutability of being, man must possess two widely different capacities, one for perceiving different and changing shapes, another for knowing ultimate being, i.e. sensation which makes one acquainted with the surface of things, and reason which understands the deeper essence of being. It was in this roundabout way that the ancient Greeks came to state the problem of knowledge.

Their theory of knowledge, based on a clear-cut dualism of sensation and reason, was not the result of an independent inquiry into the nature of knowing, but rather the end-product of their limited point of view concerning the problem of being which they thought could be solved by singling out one or four primeval kinds of matter. The only problem which they really considered was that of the transformation from one kind of matter to another, or the relations between the 'one' matter and its 'many' forms. It was sufficient, they thought, to explain how basic being could co-exist with variety and mutability. One cannot say they were wrong, either in searching for a primeval matter, or in positing sensation as the epistemological opposite of reason. But they were wrong in assuming that the research into a primeval matter covered the field of philosophical inquiry, and that knowing was either perception or reason, and nothing else. Their

approach to the problem of being was limited. Their research could not exhaust the possibilities of being and
knowing. It had therefore a peculiar slant, as is proved
by the absurd and inconsistent assumptions derived from it.

Two centuries after Thales, research of this kind was
brought to bear on the peculiar cultural situation which
arose out of the political conditions in Athens towards the
end of the fifth century B.C. It was an era of 'democracy',
then, as usual, degenerating to demagogy—a time when
propaganda was of paramount importance, and the ability
to persuade the populace to appoint this or that political
boss was the goal of every political activity. In consequence, no statement was presumed to have objective
value. The value and 'truth' of a statement were no more
than its capacity of attracting the votes of the witless
common people. Right and wrong were not referred
to steadfast principles, or to settled traditions. The
Sophists, who made a profession of training politicians
to acquire followers and votes, had to assume that
truth was impermanent, and to accept the philosophy
of change.

Socrates maintained, against these, that just because
sensation, feeling, opinion were variable forms of knowledge, there must exist some impersonal and permanent
knowledge (reason), otherwise no change could ever be
perceived. Socrates' polemical method was, as is well
known, that of forcing upon the adversary a certain tenet
by means of successive questions to which only one answer
could be given. In this way philosophy was expounded
in dialogues, which accorded well with the contemporary
love of the theatre. Prior to Socrates, poetry and oratory
had been the popular forms in which physical and psychological investigation was expressed. The artistically well-
balanced, dramatically arresting Socratic dialogues of
Plato gained the approval both of his contemporaries and
of posterity, even when the interest of the reader was not
primarily devoted to philosophy. Thus platonism won

enduring success not so much by its philosophical content as by being literature of the first rank.

It has never been satisfactorily decided how far Plato was indebted to Socrates for his main tenets. It is safe to assume that Socrates had maintained that though sensation of, and individual opinion about something may change, the definition, or conception, of that something is permanent and universal. This was Parmenides' theory of immutable being, as applied to human thought in particular. Was Socrates'—and Plato's—assumption really justified? Plato in his dialogues adopts Socrates' query-answer method to reach a universal definition of such things as 'virtue', 'piety', or 'knowledge'. But many of the dialogues are 'tentative'—they do not reach an acceptable definition. Socrates proves only that the definition proposed at the beginning by somebody else is wrong. This suggests that a definition should be valid for everybody, but not that such a definition can always be found. Socrates' assumption that any definition has a universal and absolute epistemological value rests on a logically uncertain basis. On some subjects (virtue, poetry, etc.) a certain number of human minds work in the same manner when they refer a large number of single cases to a common definition. It is not proved that a universally valid definition can always be reached.

Plato thought that Socrates' assumption of a universal agreement on definitions implied that knowing and knowledge possess some unique quality. It implied indeed either that every human mind works in the same way, or that there is a common object of knowledge (the 'idea') beyond the individual mind. This 'idea' is something different from the particular objects to which the definition applies. Primitive physical theories suggested to Plato that mental conceptions or objects of thought had some kind of real existence. The first Greek thinkers had devoted much speculation towards establishing sets of 'contraries', of opposite forms of being, in order to explain how everything could arise from a single primeval matter. Plato was therefore inclined to conceive his 'idea' as a form of existence, opposed to material existence but basically similar just because opposed and therefore comparable.

This dualism of material and ideal being disclosed a further difficulty. Ideal being could not possibly mix with material being. Therefore it had to have a distinct 'place', in order to be even spatially outside the material world, 'beyond and above the (material) sky'. This meant giving to ideal existence a spatial quality which was in itself something material. Plato was forced indeed into absurd statements, such as that matter can 'partake' of the ideas, that man's body may keep enclosed in itself the soul of man which is bodyless, immaterial.

So clever a thinker as Plato could not disregard these absurdities—ideas existing in space; several souls (one immaterial and another, nay two others material) working as one soul; two worlds existing side by side, one reflecting the other and yet completely different. Plato in fact did not keep faith with the dualism which still goes under his name. In his maturer years he turned from writing enthusiastic, poetic dialogues to sober, matter-of-fact investigation of philosophical problems. Although nothing of this research has come down to us, we can see in some of his later dialogues the slow process of his investigations. In the *Sophist* he attacks those who (like he himself at an early stage) accepted the existence of a separate world of ideas. In the *Timæus*, written under the influence of Pythagoreanism, he considered the material world as subject to mensuration, and maintained that the ideal element was no more than the measurable aspect of matter.

Plato's own criticism of his earlier conceptions did not bear fruit in the further development of philosophical thought. Nobody was aware of the evolution of his thinking. His dialogues were arranged by his commentators according to their subject-matter, and not according to the successive stages of his thought. Platonists accepted as fundamental the idealistic dualism which was only the first, inchoate stage of his thought. It had been expounded indeed in the most readable dialogues. Not until a century ago did scholars attempt to sort out the different stages of Plato's thought. Hermann, Natorp, Gomperz and Jaeger arranged Plato's dialogues according to the time of their composition, so that a true understanding of the changing conceptions of the philosopher was made possible. For the twenty-two previous centuries, when European scholars spoke of 'Platonism' they meant by it only the absurd theory of an idealistic dualism which Plato himself had finally refuted and rejected.

Aristotle, Plato's pupil, advanced even further from the belief in idealistic dualism. In his effort to unify both being and thought, which had been forcibly separated by 'official' Platonism, Aristotle was forced to take into consideration a very dangerous outgrowth of Socrates' teaching—the attempt by the so-called Megaric school (and particularly by Diodoros Chronos) to account for possibility, as contrasted with actual being. It is not certain what Diodoros really meant. From an allusion of Aristotle and some hints of Cicero and Sextus one can conclude that Diodoros maintained that all that is possible is also real. Probably Diodoros meant that our thought is co-extensive with reality. Whatever was thought of as possible existed somewhere, even if outside the sphere of actual experience. In other words: our thinking of something as possible, and not yet real, implied the existence of a world of possible beings. This belief restored the two worlds of Plato—one of actual physical existence, the other of possibilities which were in a sense an intermediate being between the physical and the ideal. Aristotle who, in his revulsion from the Platonic school in which he had been trained, denied a separate ideal existence, nevertheless accepted a sort of dualism by admitting possible being as distinct from actual being.

In order to explain the existence of many kinds of material being, and the unity of the world, Platonism had been compelled to postulate a semi-divine being, the great Craftsman, who belonged to both worlds at once, and who could model matter in imitation of the Ideas. Aristotle wished to explain the genesis of individual things and the order of the world without admitting a completely distinct ideal reality, and a hypothetical Craftsman. He therefore assumed that potential being was not merely conceptual potentiality, the idea of something possible, but was indeed something real, already existent in nature. The genesis of individual things from potential to actual existence was a gradual process due only to movement and not the deliberate, manifold activity of a Craftsman. A seed was actually a seed but at the same time it was a potential tree.

In this way the grossest absurdities of Platonic dualism were eliminated, yet enough dualism remained in Aristotle's system to nullify its claims to scientific validity. If a certain thing actually existing (say, a stone) can be transformed into different things (a statue, a missile, a part of a building etc.), so that the stone itself is potentially many different things, the nature of its potential being can be seen only when it has disappeared in order to become a determinate actual existence. Therefore according to Aristotle any knowledge is, in a sense, 'wisdom after the event', and one must again admit something supranatural, another kind of Craftsman who chooses between different potentialities, and directs accordingly the growth of a thing from the potential to the actual, so that it may fit into the general order and scheme of our coherent cosmos. The genesis of any single thing had to be explained on the basis of what an intelligent Craftsman or God meant to attain, and not as a play of blind natural forces and laws, acting mechanically. This stone, in short, has become actually a stumbling block in my path instead of a statue or a building only because of the say-so of an extraneous will. This makes everything very easy to explain, but the explanation is rather meaningless. When something comes into being, it means that this something had already been there from the beginning. The early dilemma between change and immutability was overridden but not solved.

This account of the 'history' of Greek philosophy from Thales to Aristotle may seem disrespectful slander of admired geniuses to whom, in every epoch, European culture referred as to masters and teachers: Platonism and Aristotelianism are still living philosophies. But this paradoxical survey goes to prove that there was no internal necessity underlying the passage of Greek thought from Thales to Aristotle. Each successive step aimed only at solving a certain difficulty which arose from the preceding step, and the new step produced again further difficulties. Each single step is logically obvious. A 'history' which considers all the steps as connected into a coherent, developing whole (the 'History of Greek Philosophy') results from poetic interpolation only.

From the very beginning there was a bias, a one-sided approach to the problem of being—Thales' theory. None of the Greek philosophers attempted a really new departure, and none succeeded in eliminating the basic difficulties of Thales' approach. If such thinkers of genius as Plato and Aristotle could not succeed in this task to their satisfaction and ours, it is permissible to suggest that Thales' approach, and therefore the approach of all Greek philosophers, might have been unsound. The nature of being needs be investigated in some other, completely different way. It may be that here and there, in Greek philosophies, some sound points have been made, and may be taken up again fruitfully, but no Greek 'system' of philosophy as a whole, nor the 'history' of Greek philosophy, should be taken as a trustworthy guide to an investigation of being.

One can stop here instead of detailing the further steps tried by the Epicurean and the Stoic and the Neo-platonist, beginning from one or other of the great Greek philosophers. The impact of Christianity on the Western world did not change this situation, nor inspire philosophers to start anew, to search for a new approach. The dreary story went on. Platonism and Aristotelianism and Neo-platonism with all their inconsistencies were taken up again and again as they stood. Philosophers tried again and again to patch up the major discrepancies. Their successive steps in the wrong direction became even less original, and were slanted in a more inaccurate way by having to account for Christian dogma, which introduced a further basic contradiction besides the old difficulties.

Pagan philosophers were consistent at least in their conception of what means to use to solve the problem of being. It was a matter for reason and experiment, a rational approach. There was no other method of knowing. The Christian philosopher, on the other hand, had to take account of Revelation and faith—another, extra-human source of knowledge. The solution of philosophical problems had to satisfy both reason and faith. An attempt was first made to proceed in the old way, to submit faith to reason, or to rationalize faith, to the imminent danger of Christianity itself—a danger which recurred again and again later. The first Christians who tried to 'think out' the Message in the cultural terms to which they were used, maintained that philosophical Christianity was another Christianity, a church of the intelligentsia, the Gnostic church. The earliest Fathers of the Church had to fight Gnosticism in order to avoid the reduction of Christian faith to a spineless philosophy. The successful attempt of Clement and Origen to build up a Christian gnosis (a philosophy which would not alter the fundamental lines of Jesus' teaching) brought the contrast of reason and faith into the internal structure of Christian philosophy. A most evident sign of internal contradiction is the teaching of Christian churches on man's survival after death. The (Platonic) idea of an immortality of the soul is accepted side by side with the (Jewish-Pharisaic) belief in the resurrection of the body.

The struggle of the European mind to reconcile these contradictions went on throughout the Middle Ages. No effort was made towards finding a new point of departure, not even towards a development of those philosophical positions which had been left half-shaped by Greek thinkers. Philosophical research aimed rather at reconciling the provisional results of primitive thought, with the faith which had arisen independently, out of another cultural tradition.

An attempt at a new start was made at the beginning of the 17th century. Although it too was influenced by ancient ideas, it can be considered as 'modern' philosophy. The 'history of modern philosophy' is a description of efforts to overcome difficulties inherent in a new, but still unsound, approach. Even in this case, as in that of Thales, the approach, the bias was not philosophical. While Thales, in brief, had considered the problem of being from the standpoint of a religious myth, modern philosophers approached philosophy from the standpoint of a modern myth—the mythical absolute value of science.

The accumulated discoveries and observations of natural science made the new age superior to ancient Greece in the number of its scientific notions. This 'advance' so entranced philosophers that they attempted to base philosophical research on scientific principles, and to search for a philosophical interpretation of scientific methods. The starting point of modern philosophy was therefore directly connected with scientific conceptions as they prevailed at the beginning of the 17th century. Bruno had revived ancient pantheism and mystical tendencies within the framework of a general interpretation of Copernican astronomy. Bacon thought that philosophy should be a scientific encyclopaedia. Descartes presented his philosophy as a methodical introduction to his scientific treatises.

The most advanced sciences of the early 17th century were physics and mathematics. They were considered as sciences *par excellence*, and all other forms of research tended to adopt physico-mathematical methods. Modern philosophy did likewise. No one seems to have questioned the efficacy of scientific methods for philosophical research. Moreover, since modern philosophies were based on science, they should have changed step by step with the changes or improvements in physico-mathematical theories and methods. If this had happened, it would at least have substantiated the contention of the historicist that there is a steady development, and that history is a lineal growth in all fields. This did not happen. Whilst science was developing, philosophers adhered to the original point of departure and continued to patch up, step by step, both the difficulties inherent in it and those which appeared through the attempts of their predecessors to correct earlier absurdities. Once again, as in ancient Greece, every philosopher was related to one or more philosophers whom he tried to correct or to controvert— a set of fitful, occasional individual connections masquerading as 'history' of modern philosophy, which is in fact only a succession of philosophers and a succession of steps without any common spirit but a blind devotion to a starting point already obsolete. The latest results of science were interpreted on the basis of philosophical principles borrowed from the earliest conceptions of modern science. Modern philosophy and modern science grew progressively apart, with ludicrous results—Hegel's theoretical account of natural facts, so fantastic in an epoch when new sciences such as chemistry, thermodynamics, etc.,

E

were coming to the fore—Schopenhauer's interpretation of the positive results of modern biology on the basis of a philosophical theory which derived from Kantian data, etc.

The artless attitude of modern philosophers towards science becomes evident to anybody who reads Edmund Husserl's last work, *Die Krisis der Wissenschaften*. According to Husserl, modern science as developed by Galileo and taken up by Descartes as a basis of his philosophy implies that nature must be explained mathematically. Galileo stated that God had written the innermost meaning of nature in a language made of figures and geometrical patterns. Whilst, according to the ancient (Pythagorean, Platonic) conception, physical nature only 'participated' in ideas and numbers, modern science believes nature to be mathematical in its very essence. Modern scientists idealize nature in a geometrico-mathematical pattern. Qualitative differences disappear. Only metrical, i.e. measurable qualities remain. Natural research is not a description of facts but a reduction of facts to a mathematical skeleton. Therefore our sensations (i.e. nature as it appears to us) are not related intimately to what is believed to be scientific 'truth' about nature. The world appears to us as a context of qualities but science assumes that its reality is metrical, i.e. that it is made of different quantities and of measurable geometrical patterns of some uniform element (atoms, matter). According to the views of the early 17th century, science 'explains' the world by describing its infinite qualitative variety as being no more than different quantities of matter and movement. Therefore the world of modern science, of Galileo and Descartes, is a self-enclosed unity. There is absolutely nothing else in the physical world but these two measurable elements: nondescript matter and movement in different quantities. Qualities as perceived by us—and therefore even our mind (which yet must have something to do with this mathematical world as it knows it)—do not have any

place in it. Mind would introduce into the physical
world, as known by modern science, qualities which
science must ignore because science deals only with
metrical reality.

Therefore, according to Descartes, mind (and thought)
had to be studied as a reality apart, a being in itself,
'outside' the world of physical science. Mind and thought
are a world in themselves, a world parallel and similar to
that of matter, yet completely exclusive and self-contained. Descartes tried indeed to construct the manifold
realities of thought on a mathematical pattern, similar to
the metrical-geometric one of natural science. Thinking
in all its forms had to be based ultimately on a single
element which corresponded to the single material element of the physical world. The single element of Descartes' world of thought was not an activity but a being,
a basic stuff: the I, the self-consciousness. In this way
there arose the celebrated Cartesian 'dualism' of mind
and matter, of *res cogitans* as against *res extensa*. This
dualism became the fundamental assumption of modern
philosophy. No 'modern' philosopher ever seems to have
been aware that the scientific conceptions on which
Descartes' dualism rested had been rejected by science
itself almost immediately after Descartes' own time.

(1) The early 17th century thinkers, in conceiving
physical events, referred them to movement, as Aristotle
had done. Mechanics covered the whole realm of physics.
But science went on enquiring about the *cause* of movement, with the result that the concept of force (dynamics)
became the real subject of physical research. Later still
force was no longer considered so unique as to justify a
purely metrical interpretation of nature. Scientists advanced the conception of manifold energies, and then
of many 'atoms' of action, which completely superseded
mechanics as a sufficient explanation of the world.

(2) Descartes, by conceiving of matter merely as some-

thing which occupied a certain amount of space, an extended thing, had attempted to reduce physics to metrical geometry. Gravitation destroyed this simple scheme. Matter was found to be not only extended but 'heavy' so that another element or quality had to be introduced into the tidy physical world of Descartes. Philosophers, however, continued to assume that matter and extension were the same. The great modern philosopher, Kant, a century and a half after Descartes and a century after Newton's discovery, still assumed that the very concept of matter included extension but did not include weight and gravitation.

(3) Even in our own times, one finds contemporary philosophy still discussing Descartes and his successors, still assuming (as did Newton and Kant) that absolute space and time are a prerequisite of science and therefore are to be considered by philosophy, although it has been proved by Einstein that a practically sound scientific description of the world cannot be elicited but by assuming that time and space are relative.

The unsoundness of the starting point of modern philosophy should have been apparent to Descartes himself, or at least to his immediate successors. Dualism, which was the unavoidable result of philosophical allegiance to the methods and principles of early modern science, should have induced philosophers to throw away Descartes' philosophy and to search for another point of departure. Instead they went on attempting to mend Descartes, and this dismal progress from old to new difficulties has been considered as a progress and has been called 'history' of modern philosophy.

On the face of it Descartes' dualism was absurd. If the material and spiritual worlds are unrelated forms of being, they cannot possibly be connected. It is then impossible to explain how a material cause (say, a light, a sound-wave, a movement) can produce a spiritual effect (a sensation)—and how a spiritual event (an idea, a

feeling) may bring forth a material event, e.g. a movement of our body. Descartes himself offered the ludicrous hypothesis that the pineal gland in our brain was a
point of contact between mind and body. Cordemoy,
Geulincx and Malebranche maintained that as reciprocal
action between mind and body was impossible, material
and spiritual events corresponded one to another owing
to a direct action of God himself. In this way they gave
up the basic rule of modern 'positive' science—that nature
should be explained without any reference to extra-
natural causes. Cleverer solutions (such as Spinoza's reduction of spiritual substance and material substance to
two *attributes* of a single substance, or Leibniz' pre-
established harmony) did not put philosophy on the right
path because most probably the right path is to be found
in some other direction.

Even those philosophers who, though more or less
independent of Descartes, were still under the spell of
modern science, felt bound to accept a dualistic conception
of being. Hobbes reduced thought to a movement of
matter, and considered psychology as a branch of physical
science. He found it impossible however either to prove
the existence of matter from a psychological standpoint,
or to explain thought-processes on the basis of physical
laws. Later on English empiricism, because its starting
point was sensation (which is a spiritual happening), was
unable to prove the existence of external reality. Locke
explained how the idea of matter arose, but he was not
able to throw a bridge between the idea and the existence
of matter. To Berkeley therefore it seemed justifiable to
state that the existence of an external world is an unwarranted assumption, and Hume thought that it was
not possible to advance beyond psychological occurrences
(impressions) which arise in our mind why and how one
does not know.

The absurdities with which modern science, in its early

years, endowed 'modern' philosophy included a mistaken conception even of the object and aims of philosophical research. Scientists dealt with the physical world only, a context of extension and movement and nothing else. As this world did not include thought and as thought was another world perfectly sufficient unto itself, philosophers came to think that the proper subject of their research was the world of thought, i.e. thinking and knowing to the exclusion of everything else. The specific problem of philosophy was no more the nature of being in general. Not even man as an intimate blend of mind and body, as it had been for Plato, for Aristotle, and for all pre-modern philosophers. Modern philosophy was basically an analysis of knowing. Everything else, even being, was examined epistemologically, i.e. from the point of view of a research into the nature of thought.

An artless justification was offered for this one-sided conception of philosophy: that the study of knowing should come before the study of being, because before eliciting the nature of being, one should understand how being is known. But this argument can be easily reversed by observing that the thinker who assumes that thought is the object of his research, must consider thought as something real, i.e. as something which exists. Therefore he must already know what 'to exist', 'to be' mean.

There is in fact no valid reason why philosophy should start from knowing rather than from being. Both the physical and the spiritual *are*, and if philosophy explores the nature of *being*, it cannot play favourites. Philosophy is forced to begin either from being or from knowing only if it accepts the unwarranted assumption that knowing and being, the spiritual and the material are two worlds apart. In fact the epistemological bent of modern philosophy was the outcome of a preconceived split in the essence of being.

Modern philosophers left the physical world to the care of science. They preferred to co-operate with non-

scientific research—literature, history, politics, etc. Historicism was a result of this trend. Both the opposition to
science on the part of idealistic philosophers, and the
blind acceptance of provisional scientific results as permanent philosophical truths, were results of the modern
epistemological conception of philosophy.

The failure of greater and lesser modern philosophers
proved that it is not possible to fulfil the task of a philosopher by this one-sided research into the nature of knowing. Both Kant and Berkeley started from an exploration
of thought, and identified thought and objective reality.
At a certain stage of the development of their epistemological philosophy, they saw the impossibility of explaining the nature of knowing in itself except by an
unexplained hypothesis about being, and by referring to
something existing, not only *thought of* as existing. To
explain the distinction between objective and illusory
thought Berkeley had to appeal to the existence of God
and to offer the inconsistent theory of a divine perception.
Kant's research into the procedure of knowing brought
him to the conclusion that human knowing was limited,
and therefore he had to assume that there is something
outside thought, something existing by itself independently of thought, which influences thought.

They tried to pursue this line further and to explore
the nature of that being introduced perforce into the
context of their epistemological philosophy. This research
forced them at a later stage to renege their earlier
epistemological assumptions and to disrupt their very
conception of knowing. From his youthful empiricism
and immaterialism Berkeley in old age somersaulted into
the rationalism and materialism of the *Siris*. Kant died
when he was about to deny (as one sees in the draft of his
last work, the *Opus postumum*) the final result of his
elaborate criticism of reason—that no objective reality
corresponds to the 'ideas' of our reason.

One might 'read' the *Critique* of Kant as a statement

about being, or rather about the nature of man, according to the existentialist interpretation of Heidegger. This **does** not correct Kant's epistemological metaphysics. But Kant himself believed he was still inquiring about knowing alone when as a matter of fact he had already reneged the methods and results of his *Critique*.

Then the epistemological preconceptions of modern philosophy led to the 'idealism' of Kant's immediate successors: Fichte, Schelling, Hegel. Seeing that the blind alley of epistemology offered no way out towards being, they drew being into the blind alley itself (so to speak), by supposing that any kind of being is a transmogrification of pure thought or of rationality in general. They thought that in this way an epistemological approach to the problems of philosophy could be justified. There was still something to be justified—the basic assumptions of modern philosophy. Were they really unavoidable?

The unsatisfactory nature of idealism was shown by the opposition of the positivist. Idealist against realist, positivist against historicist. No peace then for modern philosophy which stands condemned to the internal inconsistencies of each philosopher and to a perpetual quarrel between opposing acceptations of its initial mistake.

This summary review seems to substantiate the initial contention that history of philosophy does not prove an evolution or an advance of the human mind and of its understanding of the innermost nature of being. There is no 'history' of philosophy in the sense more or less consciously accepted even by the greatest philosophers.

A careful weighing of the evidence makes one doubt whether there may have been an overall development, or even a consistent advance within the limits of a particular 'school' of philosophical thought, i.e. a progress of idealism or of empiricism or of realism from some early idealists, etc., to the latest ones. What is immediately apparent, is that philosophers always differ, even within the same school of thought. There appears only change—which is not progress in itself—in the mind of the single philosopher, and in the succession from one to another. This may mean only that philosophers have had to try and make consistent a philosophy which could not possibly be consistent. The underlying force compelling philosophers and schools of philosophy to change, both throughout the ages and during their individual life, is the force of logic. When a philosopher looks deeper into his own assumptions, or explores some problem he had not previously taken into account, and finds an inconsistency, he cannot just sit down and say blandly that the principle of non-contradiction and the rule of consistency are obsolete and overrated. Mind can work only if it thinks consistently. Inconsistent thought is no thought at all.

Therefore histories of philosophy and monographic studies of individual philosophers are philosophically relevant only if they are read backwards. Changes in the course of the 'history of philosophical thought', changes from the first meditations to the death of a philosopher, prove that philosophers have discovered inconsistencies in their thought or in the philosophy of their predecessors, and in trying to overcome them, have had to shift their position. Had they ever been confronted with a monolithic system of thought, in their own or their predecessor's mind, they would never have enquired further.

This proves that the starting point of any great line of thinkers referring one to another ('history of ancient philosophy', 'history of modern philosophy', and 'schools of philosophy' as Platonism, empiricism, etc.) and the starting point of each single philosopher who has hitherto appeared on the stage, have been unilateral. All starting points hitherto tried have proved wanting.

Therefore, by reading backwards the 'evolution' of a school and of a thinker, we may discover the original bias, and the primitive problem considered, and dismiss them as philosophically unsound. The very changes, which seem to constitute a 'history of philosophy', suggest that we should avoid every opening hitherto explored so as to be able to find by elimination some completely new starting point. This is the only lesson a would-be philosopher can learn from other philosophers and from the so-called 'history of philosophy'.

# CHAPTER III

# MARX AND THE GOLDEN AGE

The mode of production of the material means of
life conditions in general the social, political and
spiritual process of living.

MARX, *Critique of Political Economy*

THE ARBITRARY CONSTRUCTION which is put upon facts when they are described and ordered as historical events is largely influenced either by the rose-coloured or by the gloomy outlook of the historian. It was seen in the preceding chapter that a history of human thought as a connected whole can be written only by an optimist, proud of the rational quality of man, and sure of his conquests. He believes that philosophy advances unceasingly towards truth, that the power of human thought is evidenced by great thinkers who have attained at least a partial knowledge of ultimate reality.

When however the historian tries to give an account not only of speculative thought, but of civilization in general, the resulting 'philosophy of history' is not always ruled by an optimistic outlook. Up to World War I, Progress was taken for granted. To doubt the gradual improvement of mankind would have been regarded as subversive. In classical times, on the contrary, the course of mankind had always been described in terms of an original Golden Age from which mankind had progressively degenerated.

It is interesting to note that the prevalence of optimism or pessimism in a certain epoch does not always seem due to the actual prosperity or unhappiness of that epoch. Poets of the Augustan age of Rome, proud and assured as they were of her attainments and glory, still believed that mankind had degenerated from a previous happier state. Today we live uncomfortably under the shadow of H-bombs, and yet we are somehow proud of our science, which has 'progressed' so much as to be on the verge of destroying mankind and the world.

In claiming that the Golden Age myth was the common faith of the ancient, Progress that of the modern, we do not mean that every thinker or writer of note was

68

then a pessimist, and is now an optimist. Philosophies of history, like systems of philosophy, are inherited. A historian of recent times may be influenced by some classical writer, and accept his pessimistic outlook. Tasso, for instance, at the close of the Renaissance, adopted the Golden Age ideology because he re-echoed classical pastoral poetry which used as its background the dreamland of Arcadia, a representation of human society in Golden Age conditions. Slightly before Tasso, there were late humanists who doubted whether civilization contributed to human happiness: the unruly savage of Golden Age times, the primitive shepherd of Arcadia, were perhaps less unhappy and less dishonest.

Nor was this only an effect of the Renaissance and of its retrospective attitude. In the 18th century also, when the Progress superstition was already a common faith, Rousseau and many others took up again the ancient complaint. The general disgust with European society, the craze for exploration and discovery, made many turn to the 'noble savage' as a paragon of the 'good' life. Later still, one finds cases of a reaction against Progress, but they were few and far between, so that a pessimist like Morris seems to have been out of step with his age. Only in our own day do we see the myth of Progress slowly and reluctantly crumble when confronted by overpowering evidence of general unhappiness and moral rottenness.

However, we can state broadly that a pessimistic philosophy of history was as common in ancient times as an optimistic hope in the future has been in the last two centuries. This is clear if we consider the practical issues involved in and evolved from the Golden Age myth, compared with the Progress superstition. According to the latter, there is no need to try and steer the chariot of history in a particular direction. Simply by going on mankind advances towards ever-greater well-being and higher attainments. The Golden Age ideology suggested instead that we should stop the course of history and go

back, begin anew—in a sense, try to reach the past instead of the future. It was, and it is, a very practical
issue, perhaps the most relevant practical problem in any
epoch. Is revolution or reaction the best policy for improvement? Is the old or the young man an ideal type of
the world-wise Sage?

Anyway, if it is true that the ancient commonly
believed in regress, and the modern in progress, how
did this great change of opinion occur, in the course
of a civilization like the European? (This 'course' does
not imply a 'history' of Western Europe. It is a succession
only because any European thinker and artist is influenced by European thinkers and writers who lived before
him.) How did it come to pass that this heritage, this
sequence, was interrupted and at a certain moment
pessimism was superseded by optimism?

Between the modern world and the ancient, Europe
had been subjected to the impact of Christianity. It came
from outside—a Message from on High. But let us avoid
this matter-of-fact statement which might hurt the
feelings of our 'scientific humanists'. Let us put the
matter as they can understand it, according to their historical superstititions, and say that it was the impact of a
foreign (Jewish) civilization which brought into ours such
ideas (now of course 'obsolete') as sin, the Fall, and a need
of redemption.

Christian 'philosophy of history' is by no means indifferent as between ancient pessimism and modern optimism. It is in fact ambivalent. In it we find again the
Golden Age myth—Adam in Eden—and a final improvement at the very end—the Kingdom of God. There
is no gradual decadence: man 'fell' down all the way at
once; nor is there a 'progress' towards final well-being:
this will be realized suddenly. Between the Fall and the
Millennium, there can be neither decadence nor progress.
Evil is an actual presence, from the beginning to the very
end. Mankind lives in a state of siege, as a militant

Christian community. No steps forward or backward can really be made by mankind or society as such. On the other hand, the eternal destiny of each single man is his own destiny, and not the destiny of his society or race or nation or civilization.

This teaching broke the ancient tradition. Even amongst Christians lonely voices were heard which either recalled a happier past, or dreamt of a happier future. But Christian opinion was sure that there could be, for man, no change either for better or worse. One had to fight step by step, and no step was easier than the former or the next—evil was present, unchangeable, in our innermost essence, in the very texture of society. Instead of trying to 'improve' society, the Middle Ages tried to freeze it, to crystallize it into a fixed hierarchy of classes and duties which could best resist evil: the warriors, the learned, the labourers—the social order of an armed camp, awaiting the last trump.

Such was the common, Christian 'philosophy of history' of the Middle Ages. At the end of them, there was a brief resurgence of classical pessimism and of the Golden Age myth. The Renaissance man believed his age had decayed, and hoped for an improvement by being 'born anew'—by returning to the golden times of Greek and Roman civilization. When the Renaissance heritage was swept away in the 17th century by an increased interest in science, the so-called 'free thinking' impeded a return to mediaeval standards. There was ample scope for a reaction both against ancient pessimism and Christian tradition—for an optimistic 'philosophy of history', a product of man's blind pride and pleasure in discoveries and inventions—for the superstition of Progress.

As was said above, the superstition is slowly retreating in our time before hard realities and the desperate situation of mankind. Yet the contemporary mind is still haunted by a number of ghosts fathered by Progress in the heyday of its power. To exorcise them, it will be

necessary to understand the Progress myth and its rami-
fications by comparing it to the now forgotten myth of a
Golden Age.

Indian sages too spoke of a fatal decadence of mankind
through four successive stages. But our European tradition, as expressed by Roman poets of the Augustan age,
finds its literary origins in Hesiod.

According to him, the immortals who live in the houses
on Olympus created a golden race of men who got fruits
from the earth with little exertion, and lived and died in
peace, distributing labour and products on a communal
basis. Then came a silver generation, and men swiftly
grew insolent and forgot the Gods. Zeus swept them
away and created a third breed, the bronze race, with
houses and walls, and hearts too, of bronze, which de-
lighted in fighting and warfare. Then came a fourth
race, a better one, more virtuous and just than the third:
the age of the great Greek heroes and of the Trojan war.
Hesiod indeed was not able to resist the charm of old
songs and mighty deeds, and supposed that in this fourth
age decay had paused. It was a new spring of mankind,
but it did not last. The fifth age, the age in which the
poet himself lived, was, he said, an age of iron. Men had
discovered the use of iron and their very souls were of
iron:

> . . . never in the day
> Cease labour and tears, never in the night
> Do we escape fear: the Gods give us
> Heavy sorrows. . . .

Greek and Hellenistic poets took up the sad burden.
Ovid still reproduced Hesiod's conception of human history. Virgil, the national poet of imperial Rome, placed
the Golden Age in Latium, in the territory near to Rome:

> Saturn came first from ethereal Olympus,
> Flying from Jove and his arms, losing his kingdom.
> Unruly mankind, dispersed on the high mountains,

He did order and submit to laws, and called the place
'Latium' because there men lay concealed in safety.
Under this king it is said there were golden
Ages. So he ruled peoples in becalmèd peace,
Till a worse and stained age slowly succeeded
And warring fury and love of possessions.

According to Juvenal mankind has lost not only virtue
but even physical comeliness and stature:

At the age of Homer already was this race becoming smaller:
Now on the earth grow only small and ungodly men,
So that any God who sees them, laughs at and despises them.

This implies in a sense a natural degeneration of mankind. Hesiod had proposed also a moral explanation
by averring that unhappiness, painful labour, difficult
existence and internecine fighting were the consequences
of some transgression against the Gods.

This point of view possibly derived from Mesopotamic
sources. A grievous blunder or sin excluded man from
the secluded safety and peace of a blessed enclosure where
he, a food-gatherer, got everything for nothing. He was
thrown out into the wide world where he could not gain
his bread but by cruel toil. Murder and war began at
once.

The Golden Age myth appears today as a poetic dream
without any possible relation to factual events. Yet some
of the main ideas of this ancient story have been re-stated
by contemporary scientists. Social science maintains that
the dawn of civilization and the beginnings of cultivation
were connected just as the ancient myth supposed them
to be. Saturn created the Golden Age by teaching lawful
order and agriculture to Janus; when the Golden Age in
Eden ended, Adam became a food-producer, and his son,
a typical agriculturist or food-producer, formed the first
society, 'built a city', after overcoming Abel, the representative of a more primitive pastoral society.

It is true that according to the Pagan version the

F

Golden Age was coeval with the beginnings of social life and agriculture, whilst according to the Hebraic version the Golden Age had ended when agriculture and social life began. The chronological divergence is not however relevant to the purpose. As a matter of fact agriculture and society were the result, not of a single invention but of a gradual development. The prophet and the poet (the primitive historian and sociologist) liked clear-cut outlines. They attributed to a single inventor, and gave an exact date to, slowly unfolding phenomena. They came therefore to differ about dating, as our historians differ when they try to fix the time-limits of the Renaissance, of capitalism, of the Roman Empire, etc. Nevertheless, according to Hesiod and Virgil, to Indian and Jewish sages, social life began when mankind passed from the food-gathering stage (hunting wild game, gathering of wild fruits, roots, etc.) to the food-producing stage (breeding of domesticated animals, cultivation of grains, etc.). Modern sociologists accept this point of view. Some of them accept even the ancient theory, that war was an invention of civilized beings.

There were, of course, human groups and cultures even before agriculture, but a fully developed, legally systematized, rationally planned society—a 'society' in our modern sense—could be formed only against an agricultural background. Tillage requires fixed settlements and some scientific knowledge: astronomical reckoning of time, elementary botany, etc. Some modern sociologists indeed have observed that primitive species of grain, from which our wheat and other edible grains were evolved, can be found as a wild, spontaneous growth in the highlands which overshadow the Nile and Tigris-Euphrates valleys, the oldest seats of civilizations comparable to ours.

It might well be that an elaborate civilization could thrive on the economic basis of food-gathering. But no such civilization is known to us. The oldest Middle East and Greek civilizations were food-growing, and the Golden Age myth refers to the conditions of a civilized society as they were known to ancient writers. Agriculture by itself meant a great change indeed, and ancient scholars well knew it. Dicearch, a disciple of Aristotle, divided the social history of ancient Greece into three periods: barbarism (food-gathering), nomadic life (flock-tending), agricultural civilization.

Let us now compare that ancient myth to the superstitious belief in a steady improvement of human conditions. This belief was not the result of a traditional knowledge of past events, but expressed only factually unjustified hopes, fostered by the polemical position assumed by 'enlightened 'thinkers opposed to the ideals of the Middle Ages. The strong social sense of the Middle Ages had been disrupted by the impact of Renaissance individualism, with its implication that one's only duty was to develop, to cultivate, to enrich oneself. Mankind as a whole was not important. Individual gifts and attainments were of paramount value. 'Capitalism', so-called, was the economic expression of individualism. Modern States and absolute kingship were its political aspects. The Renaissance was the passing glamour of its ideals of beauty and of an over-evaluation of the artist's personal activity. This individualism involved a social deterioration which was keenly evidenced when the general economic crisis of the second half of the 16th century ended, in unparalleled despondency, the brief age when mere beauty and individual effort were the aims.

Upon 17th and 18th century thinkers fell the task of justifying the desertion of mediaeval ideals. Modern times had one attainment only to show against increasing evils and destitution: the new science, with its marvellous discoveries and useful inventions. It was therefore proclaimed that new science had been made possible only by sweeping away mediaeval ways of thinking. Modern art was extravagantly praised not only in comparison with mediaeval art (which began to be defamed as 'gothic', i.e. barbaric and unruly) but even as superior to that classic art and literature which had been praised by Renaissance critics. The Christian conception of history, according to which only God knows the real course of events underlying the apparent course of history, was superseded. Modern man would have none of that Christian scepticism about our real knowledge of history. He believed that history as he saw it (or rather as he wished it to be) was the witness of truth.

As a matter of fact, a general survey would have proved that there was nothing to be proud of in modern conditions after the Renaissance. Social evils were as bad or worse than in the Middle Ages. Literature and fine art were meant to astound by novelty rather than to enrapture by beauty. All this was disregarded. Like a child in a toy-shop, modern man was enthralled by the unlimited vistas opened by modern science and amused by the discovery of useful gadgets and complicated engines. He did not look all around. Having only the scientific fair-ground in sight, he believed mankind had really come a step further and higher than in past times, by accumulating a lot of small inventions and one-sided researches. 'Scientific' thought, experiment, mathematical theorizing and free thinking were the rage, and the pride, of modern man. Later on, in the 19th century, the strange theory of evolution provided a further reason for believing in progress. Man had begun as a fish and a monkey. What a marvellous conquest, to breathe in the air and to do without a tail! Between decayed angel and evolved ape, modern man sided with the ape. A comparison with the angel would have proved his lowly state. He looked at beasts as his true forefathers, and felt he had improved unmeasurably. By standing on a heap of engines and accumulated wealth he imagined himself taller and 'better' than any other possible being.

What was meant by 'better'? A better beast? or a better mind? Better as to his morality, or as to his weapons? Better because happier, or because more troubled by 'better' insight into the puzzles of being and living? Nobody really asked whether by improving one side, one had perhaps ruined another side of life and society. As men lived in a later age, they supposed they had 'gone on' in the course of history. They had accumulated experience and wealth, therefore they were certain of having progressed from the ancient and mediaeval state.

When there is no settled faith, no settled standards, there is nothing to counter the psychological effects of novelty. When a new discovery, a new invention is produced, everybody is interested and charmed, and thinks: 'In older times *this* was not known! I am indeed "better" than my ancestors. Poor chaps! They could not fly. They could not kill more than one or two people at a shot. . . . ' Modern man fell a prey to this illusion. 'Later' and 'better' were for him synonymous. His attention was turned to the new—he did not see what of the old was disappearing, nor ask whether something of the old was perhaps worth preserving. The novelty-craze went so far that destruction was seen with complacent pleasure—destruction of many forms of life to provide a clear field for evolution, destruction of human types and classes to clear the way of social progress.

As a matter of fact, man has to pay for any kind of change—to give up something so as to get something else. Progress at its best is one-sided, it implies the decay and death of something else. We could be sure that by changing we had not struck a fool's bargain only if we had a permanent, universal yardstick on which to measure whether what we get is better than what we have to give up. The only acceptable standard of 'better' and 'worse' for mankind should be an absolute value.

This can only be the happiness and morality of mankind. And indeed the Golden Age myth was stated in these terms of greater and lesser happiness and virtue. From Progress-devotees we hear more often of 'civilized life', of 'social justice', of cultural and social improvement as absolute standards, unrelated to happiness and morality. A 'just' society may not be happier than a feudal society. The diffusion of culture implies that everybody must be *forced* to undergo a course of instruction even if he personally does not think that illiteracy is an unmitigated evil.

Attempts at referring Progress to happiness have been very few. We can only quote a distinctive conception of utilitarianism, that of Bentham, and of a few of his predecessors and followers, who measured the relative merits of different societies and constitutions on the standard of the principle of utility,

which approves or disapproves of every action whatsoever according to the tendency which it appears to have to augment or diminish the happiness of the party whose interest is in question.

Formerly, Bacon had hailed scientific discoveries because he thought they could produce satisfactory conditions of life, and therefore a greater happiness. But modern sociologists do not usually accept utilitarian standards. They deem Bentham a rather disreputable Epicurean. Social equality must be fostered even if it has nothing to do with 'the greatest happiness of the greatest number'—a society at the lowest level of subsistence and of individual happiness can indeed be perfectly 'just'. Scientific progress must, it seems, be pursued without any regard to its cost. It is praiseworthy and admirable when it proves capable of healing our ills by penicillin as well as when it proves able to destroy mankind with H-bombs.

Since the Progress myth could show only scientific discoveries—inventions and their effect—as factual evi-

dence that today is better than yesterday, the votaries of
Progress supposed that technical improvement by itself
improves human happiness and social conditions. This
appears an unwarranted assumption. There is the story of
a king who suffered from melancholia. The Court physi-
cian told him that he could be cured only by borrowing
and wearing the shirt of a happy man. His courtiers
searched far and wide in the world for somebody who was
happy and satisfied with his state, but could find no one.
At long last they happened upon a poor peasant working
and singing in a field, who, on being asked, professed
complete happiness. But the peasant did not wear a shirt.
The stupidity of the king's doctor in thinking that a
shirt (or any material means of life) may produce happiness and well-being by itself, is paralleled by the modern
theorist who believes that technical improvements foster
'progress' in a general sense.

Happiness and well-being are spiritual conditions and
involve a psychological element. It might be contended
that 'happiness' is a very vague term, scarcely scientific.
'Well-being' cannot be measured. But this criticism
works both ways. If one cannot consider happiness and
well-being when one speaks of 'progress', then the term
'progress' applies only to ascertainable and measurable
material conditions, and cannot mean the 'progress of
mankind', of a certain people, or of a certain civilized
group.

Believers in progress may contend that, from an objective and unselfish point of view, scientific progress
implies a progress of mankind because mankind knows
more than before, even if the 'advancement of learning'
does not have any earthly use. In this statement one finds
again the argument that Bacon borrowed from mediaeval
sources. One who is later knows more because he can
draw on an increasingly accumulated store of facts and
ideas. Nevertheless, knowing more does not prove higher
intelligence or improved mental capacities. 'Advance of

learning' and 'progress of man' (as a rational being) are not equivalent.

Moreover, what do 'knowledge' and 'learning' mean? The real import of them and of their accumulation is reflected today in the increasing specialization of the scientist and the man of letters. In the past the ideal type of scientist was the poet-philosopher-scientist-physician. By increasing the available store of facts and ideas, it became necessary to resort to strict professionalism. The philosopher could no longer do the work of the scientist. The doctor could no longer be a professional thinker. The teacher could no longer find out by himself what he had to teach, but had to use records and handbooks. The accumulation of knowledge (which is a material phenomenon) could not be stopped, and the professional man has now become a specialist. Learning and science are split up more and more. Today the heart specialist does not know much about bowels. An expert anaesthetist would hardly try to lance a boil.

It will be answered that the overall knowledge of mankind as a whole is nevertheless greater; but mankind or society 'as a whole' is an absurdity in the case of specialized knowledge. Specialized knowledge cannot be partaken of by everybody, so that there is no overall learning or science. A really specialized scholar or scientist cannot understand a scholar or a scientist of another ilk. The 'advance' of knowledge splits up culture into isolated atoms of deep but peculiar knowledge. One cannot speak any more of the learning and of the scientific knowledge 'of mankind' or of a certain 'people'. It is true that available technical means are more plentiful and more differentiated. There are more books and more machines. But nobody can read all the books, nor use every machine. A library of one million volumes does not contain more knowledge than a library of one thousand books, if nobody reads them all.

All this goes to show that the Progress myth is funda-

mentally a materialistic faith. It must refer always to
what is material in order to justify its pretensions. It can
never refer progress to the mind of men. Or, it must
postulate that material or technical conditions in and by
themselves improve man's mind, improve culture, improve society, etc. That is to say, the first dogma of the
religion of Progress is historical materialism.

Historical materialism as such does not however presuppose progress. It implies only that material and
technical conditions are the cause of spiritual occurrences
—of cultural productions, of religions, of art, of social
forms, of all that is broadly meant by 'civilization' or
'cultural background'. It does not state that changed
conditions and culture are *better* conditions and culture,
as does the Progress myth. Yet historical materialism
developed from the materialistic assumptions of the Progress myth. Montesquieu prepared the way by averring
that geographic conditions (climate, etc.) conditioned
political forms of society. Before the end of the 18th
century, a Scottish professor maintained that social and
political situations were determined by the accumulation
of wealth, 'the source of influence and authority'. The
theory was further evolved by Marx, who was not however simply a votary of Progress. One cannot state
definitely whether he was a pessimist or an optimist. He
seemed rather optimistic when he attributed some moral
value to the classless society, which was to be, according
to him, the latest stage in the evolution of society. But
properly speaking, the historical materialism of Marx did
not imply improvement and progress. It stated only that
material or technical conditions of production change
more or less slowly, and by changing they alter the social
frame either slowly, or by a sudden unavoidable 'social
revolution', due to the conflict between new conditions
and the old frame of society. Culture, religion, literature,
philosophy, etc., reflect a certain social situation. History

in all its aspects is due ultimately to economic changes.

The term 'materialism' when applied to original marxism requires further qualification. Initially Marx thought
of 'matter' in an almost Hegelian sense, as a first step
towards 'spirit'. On the other hand, since technical
changes are the result of human inventions and discoveries, which are spiritual, there seems to be a circle from
the spiritual to the material, and again from the material
to the spiritual. Contemporary orthodox marxists have
dismissed these philosophical niceties. They are downright naive realists. They call 'matter' what is matter, a
being totally different from the spirit. On the other
hand, even taking 'matter' in a Hegelian sense, it comes
before the 'spirit'. And if there is a circle of causality,
material conditions cause or influence social and spiritual
occurrences at a certain stage at least.

It is to this basic postulate of marxism in all its forms
that earnest criticism should be addressed. Such criticism
involves a further development of the philosophical analysis of our conception of time which was given above in
the first chapter, and can be set forth in simple terms.

There are different kinds of time. This seemingly
paradoxical tenet has been maintained by many philosophers of note. We have already quoted St. Augustine.
According to him man exists in time, in a succession of
past-present-future, whilst God is in eternity, and eternity is not a succession but an eternal moment, an everlasting 'now'. Bergson contrasted the time we live in,
i.e. the 'flow of our consciousness' (which cannot be
subjected to measurement) and the time of science which
is 'spread out' on space and can be measured by mechanical means. 'Speed', which can be measured only by some
fixed point of reference, implies a scientific conception of
time. One cannot on the contrary speak of a more, or
less, swift 'flow of consciousness' in itself, i.e. without
reference to some non-mental means of measurement,

such as a clock. Our consciousness moves along with the flow of our interior time, and we cannot fix a steadfast internal point of reference. When I want to remember whether I have thought of something ($A$) before or after something else ($B$), I must try to trace back the stream of consciousness to see whether in it $A$ occurred before or after $B$. When, instead, I have perceived $A$ and $B$ in the external world and seen at the same time a clock which tells me that $A$ occurred at 10 o'clock, $B$ at 11 o'clock, it is unnecessary to remember the course of my experience, to recall $A$ and $B$ as *my* experiences. I know that $A$ happened before $B$.

Because one has to use different standards to establish the succession of facts in two different kinds of time, time itself must differ in kind. In the case considered above, the 'before' and 'after' of my internal consciousness mean that this has flowed from before to after, so that their succession depends on their intimate relation, on their both being facts of the same consciousness. In the material world, however, we can fix, by using an independent point of reference, a succession between two independent and unrelated facts. I know that a certain train arrived at a London station *before* a certain ship docked at Liverpool if I am told that the hands of the clock pointed at 10 when the train arrived and at 11 when the ship docked. If I am told of the ship's docking *before* I hear of the train's arrival, and no external reference (no clock-time) is given, as far as I am concerned and my personal experience reaches, the train arrived *after* the ship had docked.

It is evident that in the cases of subjective consciousness and of external occurrences, we have to deal with two different *kinds* of time. The temporal succession of subjective experience is independent of, and unrelated to, the temporal succession of external occurrences.

The relevance of this to the question of historical materialism is evident at once. Marxism implicitly accepts

the principle of causality by stating that technical conditions govern and produce social and cultural conditions.
If however a technical change (a material, external occurrence) 'conditions' a social and cultural change, this
means that the former occurs before the latter. Marxism
therefore implies that technical and social-cultural changes
belong to the same temporal succession, i.e. that they
happen in the same kind of time.

This is a momentous error. Technical changes are external facts. The *products* of social and cultural change (a
revolution, a book, etc.) are also external facts and belong
to the same succession. But social and cultural changes *in
themselves* are human occurrences, and do not belong to
the same succession as their external manifestations. A
book may have been written and published after a book
by another author, but this is not sufficient to establish
that the first author conceived what he afterwards wrote
before the second author had thought of his book. The
cultural change in the mind of a man can happen at
any time before his decision to express it by an external
manifestation. Cultural and social changes happen in the
soul, in the mind of men, independently of their manifestations. When one has established, on external evidence, a succession of technical happenings and of cultural
or social manifestations together, one cannot conclude
that the succession of human experiences—the sequence
of feelings and thoughts in the mind of the people involved—corresponds to the succession of external facts.

There is indeed a *prima facie* case against techniques
or material facts 'conditioning' social and cultural situations. Let us now take a step nearer to reality, by considering how material conditions and human situations
are really inter-related—what, in short, is the true situation of man in regard to his material conditions, to 'the
world' in which he thinks and lives.

'To live in the world' means to exercise human activities in this world, to think and to act in it. Now, man is

a limited being. He cannot see all his world at once, he cannot use at one and the same time all the objects at his disposal. There may be in my room one or ten chairs, but I can sit only on one of them at a certain moment. I cannot walk and drive at the same time. Whilst I swallow I cannot breathe. Any human activity results from a choice between several potentialities which can be exerted, and several objects which can be used. Man's attitude to the external world, and the eventual influence upon him of technical conditions, result either from an instinctive or from a deliberate choice between available opportunities. He cannot use all of them at once. His attitude to his technical or economic world is, say, *alternative*.

Now a change of technical conditions is a *quantitative* change. If one discovers a use for some hitherto unusable material, if a new engine is invented (or if a certain food is discovered unhealthy and so eliminated from man's economic environment), then there are more or fewer external objects available. In other words, a larger or smaller number of possibilities is offered to man's choice. The 'field of choice' has been increased or decreased, and man can choose between more or fewer possibilities, but this does not mean that he can *use* more or fewer objects. He must still choose one object (or a few objects) at a time.

The votary of Progress might claim that a wider field of choice, resulting from technical and scientific 'progress', makes for a wider variety of possible choices, and therefore increases human capacities and well-being. Nothing of this kind can be assumed. As far as an increase of capacities due to an accumulation of knowledge is concerned, we have seen that the consequence of scientific development is specialization—i.e. man's possible choices in an increased field of culture become correspondingly restricted. As to an increase of well-being or happiness because of the existence of more, and more varied, goods in the world's shop, man has still to choose between them, and it is disputable whether he is happier when, his choice being limited, he must renounce a few goods which he cannot enjoy at one and the same time, or when he must give up a lot of alluring possibilities.

It might be contended that material progress improves the quality of goods (i.e. the fitness of certain goods to satisfy certain needs) and broadens the choice. Today television adds the pleasure of sight to the auditive pleasure of the wireless. Are we sure however that pleasure of sight + sound is greater than pleasure of sound only, or of sight only?—It is quite true that owing to material (economic) changes today we are not forced to choose between owning either a TV set *or* a refrigerator. We can afford both. Nevertheless, when we want a drink, we have to stop looking at TV in order to take a drink from the refrigerator. And when we are drinking and looking at the same time, are we enjoying our drink as much as if we drank without looking? Are we indeed sure we get from TV more pleasure than one of our un-civilized ancestors received from contemplating the sun-set? We cannot enjoy the sunset and TV at the same time. One might even doubt whether man, used as he is now to TV, is still able to enjoy a simple sunset.—Now we can drive or fly in a day one thousand, five thousand miles. Do we see much more than if we walked only fifteen miles?

Let us return to the general argument about historical materialism, which (as explained above) was based on the Progress superstition but is not in and by itself an opti-mistic philosophy. If material or technical conditions are changed, more or less *possibilities* of choice are available. On the other hand social and cultural conditions, i.e. human conditions, are a matter of *actual* choices. Man cannot use more (or less) things and exercise more (or less) activities at the same time only because there are more (or less) possibilities available. He is still as limited, in actual choices, as he was before a cumulative enlargement of his field, or before a restriction of it caused by decline of technical capacities or by the exhaustion of certain raw materials. The quantitative standard which is used to establish technical changes, and a temporal succession of fields of choice, cannot be applied to changes of man's choices. There is no quantitative difference between his choices. How then is it possible to claim that a certain change of human behaviour has happened—that a certain choice has been made—before or after another? Evidently the standard must be completely different from that used to establish a succession of quantitatively different fields of choice: a choice has been made before another choice because the first one came first in the flow of one's consciousness, in one's life—because the man was 'younger', nearer to his birth, when he made the first choice.

When marxism states that a change of the field of choice originates a change in the general aspect of choices themselves (i.e. in the personal, cultural, social behaviour) it should be able to affirm unequivocally that the change of the field of choice could not possibly have come after the change of choices. That is, it should establish a temporal succession of choices and of fields of choice together. How can this be done if the criterion for ordering fields in a temporal succession is quantitative, and the criterion for ordering human choices is alternative and depends on quite another consideration—on the time in which individual life flows, and of which the individual himself (and not the marxist philosopher) is aware?

This argument could, and should, be polished and refined to the limit of logical compactness. Here, one can leave it as it stands because it is sufficient to show how questionable are the assumptions of the marxist. Moreover, the present criticism goes to show that the Progress myth is so absurd that even a natural outcrop of it such as historical materialism, although it implies not progress but only change, cannot stand a rigorous philosophical check. This makes it at least permissible to return to the opposite myth, that of the Golden Age, and to enquire whether it is really so inchoate, so artless, that an adult brain should refuse it at once.

The aim of this inquiry will not be to prove that a pessimistic philosophy is more reasonable than other philosophies of history. No philosophy of history whatever is reasonable. On the contrary, it will be suggested that the Golden Age myth was logically respectable just because it was not really a philosophy of history, and did not take history into account. It was indeed a conception of man, an anthropology, based on an abstract sociological (and not historical) scheme.

Strangely enough, the point which seems most absurd in the Golden Age myth (the reference of human happiness and social conditions to the use of gold or silver or iron) is marxism *avant lettre*. The Golden Age myth claims that human morals and happiness are connected to a certain basic material, i.e. to certain 'technical means' which influence human life. Golden Age marxism however went against Marx's historical materialism by refusing to consider change, social development, in short, history. The succession of four or five ages was not a historical development. The Golden Age philosophers did not take into consideration the gradualness of inventions, discoveries and changes of life-conditions. They refused to entertain the main point of marxism, that society is in a perpetual flux which conditions both gradual changes and sudden revolutions. In the Golden Age myth one considered an 'age' as a permanent situation which did not change throughout its course, nor merge gradually into another. One age gave place to the next one by a sudden upheaval due to the action of a *Deus ex machina* or of some god-like inventor—Saturn teaching agriculture, Prometheus inventing fire, Epimetheus opening Pandora's box, Adam sinning, etc. Intellectual and moral changes were not gradual but sudden: Zeus created a new race fit to live in the new age. The universal history of

mankind was not a development but a succession of un-
connected stages. Degeneration was not a process: mankind was not coming down as it were by the chute but by
the stairs—not by a smooth sliding down but by leaps and
bounds.

Therefore, having regard to the fundamental difference between alternative choices and quantitative technical conditions, the Golden Age myth had a theoretical
compactness which is lacking in the Progress myth. It
was argued above that one cannot formulate a consistent
time-sequence of technical conditions and of human conditions. Only by avoiding the time-element (and the
Golden Age myth did this by refusing to consider an eventual development within one and the same age) can the
quantitative and the alternative be associated in a coherent
structure, and a reasonable conception of a certain type of
man in a certain kind of world be elicited. In other
words: one can describe the state of man as related to a
certain material world; one cannot explain historical evolution of man and society in connection with changing
technical conditions. The Golden Age myth was a description of different types of human life and society. It
was an abstraction because these different types never
present themselves in precisely that form, but in infi-
nitely divergent varieties, changing with time and place.
Nevertheless the historian who wishes to explain change
and describe historically the problem of civilization, cannot do it because he is not able to describe side by side, as
a coherent process, the development of technical conditions ('Progress') and of society.

The Golden Age sociologist bowed to logical consistency
when he considered certain social situations as fixed and
unchanging. On the other hand, any philosophy of
history, in its very texture, contains sociological abstractions which imply a denial of the very existence of history,
as did the Golden Age myth. Philosophers of history
(from Vico to Comte, from Spengler to Toynbee) are

G

forced to distinguish between successive ages or cycles or
civilizations through which mankind has passed, and to
describe them in their peculiarities. Vico described a
typical abstract man, the 'bestione', as a citizen of the
poetic age, etc. 'Caesarism' according to Spengler is a
general political situation which can be defined and
studied in its essence without considering that 'it happens'
i.e. it changes, it begins and develops and ends according
to a strictly 'historical' consideration. The 'challenge' of
Toynbee is the definite single effect of, for instance, a
supply of certain raw materials, even if this challenge
acts in many different ways according to the evolution of
the response to it. In short, no philosophy of history is
really able to describe a continuous development within
each age. 'Progress' or evolution or dialectical society are
not really described as growths but as fixed bulks of facts.
The golden-silver-bronze-iron ages succession as described
by the ancients was not so naive if the latest philosophers
of history can do no better. They too are sociologists
rather than historians.

Moreover, the Golden Age myth was at least able to
establish a time-sequence between 'ages', between these
bulks of sociological facts, by using a moral standard of
value. Each 'age' was above or below another because
of its value, and therefore there existed a line of development, in this case of decadence. There was a yardstick, a
moral 'clock' on which to calculate whether one age was
up or down in relation to other ages.

This is just what the sociological myths of our philosophers of history cannot do. Their 'ages', or 'cycles', or
'civilizations'—their bulks or groups of sociological facts
are all on the same level of evaluation. They are not
developing either upwards or downwards, but recurring,
repeating themselves. They succeed one to another as
one full turn of the hands on the face of the clock, or as a
revolution of the earth around the sun succeeds another.
Maya civilization and Greek civilization could have hap-

pened at any time, in fact will happen many and many times, under other names, but they will have always the very same aspect. There will be a change of challenges and therefore of response, but the laws ruling the causal connection of challenge and response will remain the same, as the law of gravitation which makes the earth turn 'again' round the sun is always the same. The so-called 'philosophies of history' are sociological abstractions which ultimately 'de-humanize' human decisions and creations by making them subject to physical laws and transferring them into the field of natural science.

The vindication of the Golden Age myth as an abstract sociological scheme makes it permissible to enquire whether some further lesson can be elicited from it. We should not forget that it was an abstraction, and therefore any conclusion drawn from it will not be factual truth but only a scientific hypothesis, valid only as all scientific hypotheses are—perhaps, to suggest practical rules of behaviour.

The bulk of facts, the 'age', is determined or identified by a certain available basic material—gold, iron, etc. The modern sociologist too speaks of old stone, new stone, bronze, iron ages. Some other scientists connotate the 'ages' according to the source of energy used—'age' of natural forces, 'age' of the steam-engine, of electricity, of nuclear energy.

Now, palaeontologists have proved that ages so defined, if one measures them on the standard of physical time, are shorter the later they are. Roughly, the old stone age lasted at least (in most places) 100-150 thousand years, the new stone age 8-10 thousand years, the bronze age 2 thousand, the iron age (when Hesiod spoke of it) was a few centuries old.—Compare on the other hand the enormous length of time during which natural sources of energy (wind, water, sun) were used before a new source (steam) was found, and the short reign of steam-power before its supersession by electricity or internal combustion, forces which are already on the wane before atomic energy.—Take another technical aspect of civilization: the speed of transportation. Before railways were invented, men had for many centuries used only animal traction and (mostly on the seas) the force of the wind. The average velocity was between 5 and 10 miles per hour, and never above 20 miles per hour. In a century or so we have now attained supersonic velocities and the average speed of transportation is now between 20 and 100 miles per hour.

It seems reasonable (within the limits of abstract science) to postulate that if we arbitrarily fix 'ages' or stages of civilization by considering a certain technical condition as their distinguishing mark, a later stage is shorter (when measured in terms of physical time) than the former. This is not strange if one remembers that technical conditions are both cumulative and interrelated. A certain improvement added to our technical powers (any quantitative enlargement of the field of choices) not only increases the technical goods available, but even their potentiality for further development. Besides, a certain technical 'world' results from complex interrelations of several technical elements. The possible number of combinations between elements increases in a geometrical ratio by each new element added, and therefore each successive invention or discovery is bound to increase in a higher ratio the number of possible combinations and the possibility of further changes.

If technical changes were an immediate cause of human behaviour (choices) and of social structures (patterns of choices), swifter technical alterations would produce in man a capacity to change more swiftly his choices and his social structures: then an increase in the rate of technical variation could be met by a greater human aptitude to change social and personal behaviour in step with the requirements of changed technical conditions.

Since technical situations are not the cause of individual choices and of social structures, swifter technical changes do not cause a swifter, more elastic adaptability of man and society.

The adaptation cannot follow a rational rule, again because there is no essential connection between material conditions and human choices. The opportune alteration of human behaviour and of social structure to meet an altered situation can only be found accidentally, by a hit-and-miss method. When the proper response has been found, man tends to perpetuate that pattern of individual and social choices which indeed makes for the highest well-being and happiness in a certain set of material conditions. A steady society, a 'people without history', could be a 'happy' people.

Our world, however, changes always. At any moment a casual discovery or the unlucky chance that a scientific genius is born, may change technical conditions. The pattern of human and social choices must be changed to meet the new situation, and a process of trial and error begins. Only repeated attempts, and then a long experience, may produce and perpetuate the best adaptation. Even if a sound knowledge of the workings of the human mind (psychology) and of human structures (sociology) could be attained, nobody could say beforehand what kind of effect might be exerted by new external conditions on human conditions. Human well-being in a technically new world can only be the fruit of experiments and experience, and therefore the pattern of individual and social life will be more or less happy according to the length of time available to try again and again, and to experiment with possible choices. Man will be able to increase individual happiness and social well-being only if he has time enough to explore possibilities. A too swift rhythm of progress limits the number of possible attempts and the length of our experience, and makes for unhappiness and social deterioration. Therefore, since technical mutability increases in process of (physical) time, happiness and well-being will continually decrease. Perhaps this is a good hypothesis to explain why no civilization has ever perpetuated itself. Its cumulative improvement in worldly riches, causing an increased ratio of change, did not allow it time enough to adapt itself to changed conditions. Unhappiness, loss of the zest to live, spiritual decay, barbarism were natural effects. Too civilized peoples are bound to disappear early because they cannot cope with their too plentiful opportunities.

The discovery of atomic energy waited for centuries. But as soon as it was made, the 'progress' from atom bomb to H-bomb was a matter of a few years. Mankind had about four centuries to try and live with gunpowder. Can one expect it will be so lucky as to hit the right behaviour in regard of atomic energy in a few years of trials and errors? 'Progress' has reached such heights that no man can live up to it. Technical improvements are bound to destroy mankind.

Of course this generalization of the Golden Age myth involves a lot of assumptions. None of them is repugnant to sound scientific methods, but science is not truth. It too refers only to technical conditions. There is something else which has not been considered here—man's moral freedom and God's omnipotence.

Within those limits, however, one must allow that the Golden Age myth contained a certain amount of social wisdom—because it was the contrary of an utopia. It appealed to direct experience when it denied that an ideal society might ever be planned. It maintained that only a certain type of man and society is good for any given set of technical conditions. Therefore it refuted the very possibility of progress. Modern Europe instead made of it a religion, and its great priest was Hegel who, in his monumental idealism, stated that Progress was God and the ultimate essence of being.

# CHAPTER IV

# RETREAT FROM HEAVEN

It is not meet for us, as many philosophers maintain, to have to do only with human things because we are men—only with mortal things because we are mortal. We should rather strive, as far as it is possible to us, to rise above death, and do our utmost to live according to the best part of ourselves.

ARISTOTLE, *Eth. Nic.*

Non v'accorgete voi, che noi siam vermi
Nati a formar l'angelica farfalla
Che vola alla giustizia senza schermi?

DANTE

THE 'GREAT SOPHIST' sat behind his high desk, clad in a blue coat with yellow buttons over a yellow waistcoat. His light blue eyes seemed to merge into the big pouches under them. His heavy jowls hung like dead flesh. The deep lines of his old face had no expression. Bent on his desk he spoke by fits and starts, pausing often to clear his throat and to take snuff, to rummage amongst the broad sheets of his notes.

Students and admirers filled the classroom. At first they could understand very little, but the oracular assurance of Hegel captured their minds. And the philosopher protected his pupils, got them appointments, formed a school in which no heretic was tolerated. His philosophy allowed him to stand well with the authorities. Formerly he had admired Napoleon, the tyrannical conqueror of his country, and had seen him as 'the Spirit of the World on horseback'. Now the Prussian state found in him a loyal supporter:

In the perfect form of the State, in which all moments of the Concept have reached a free existence, the will of the State in its subjective aspect cannot be a so-called corporate being or the decision of a majority (in which forms the unity of a deciding will has no real existence) but as a *real* individuality it is the will of One who decides, of a Monarch.

And again:

This structure as an active power is the State considered externally (objectively), which, as it has its roots in the highest essence of the State, manifests itself as State-police.

The chief attraction of Hegelianism, however, was its self-complacent optimism about the future destiny of mankind. According to Hegelianism, any form of being is in and by itself rational—being in general is 'the Idea'. Each 'position' of the Idea (each form of existence), being

96

limited, implies its contrary. The tension between affirmation and negation, between existence and nothingness
brings about their fusion, a 'synthesis' which transfers
being from that 'position' to a higher one. The 'synthesis'
indeed makes both the previous opposites more true and
real. But even this synthesis, as it is 'posited', implies the
position of a contrary—a new opposition which shall be
'superseded' by a new synthesis. Thus, being and the
world go on and on—they 'become' by an endless process.
Man is only a 'position' of the Idea, the highest point
reached by the Idea, in its limitless 'becoming'. Each
individual is the ultimate result of universal progress, and
cannot be but what he is—ultimate perfection of being.
He does not need to trouble about the destinies of mankind. Mankind goes on, ever surpassing itself beyond all
limits. Today everything is good and right because it is
the highest point reached by being. Tomorrow everything will be better. . . .

A seductive optimism indeed, even if in this way man's
individual existence, his personal problems disappear in
the immense flowing stream of the Idea.

No marvel if Schopenhauer, who for a year (1820)
tried to fight Hegel on his own ground by teaching at the
same hour, in another room of the same university,
lectured to an empty classroom. It has been told that
sometimes his only hearer was his cabby who came in to
keep warm while he waited to drive the philosopher
home.

Against Hegel's lofty optimism and rational progress,
Schopenhauer (who had just completed his greatest work)
maintained a thoroughgoing pessimism. According to
him being is not rational. The world has no logical
foundation. There is only a blind urge, an obscure Will.
This universal Will must have some object to strive for
—and must become conscious of it in its striving. The
world and the self are only 'representations', illusory
creations of this obscure urge. Any urge is, however, in

perennial conflict with itself. Any urge is suffering because it *wants* something. Both small pains and tragical
sufferings of men constitute the innermost reality of life.
Life and the world are a cosmic agony, groans of pain in
the immense void. Man is only an aching bubble on the
surface of the black pond of abysmal doom. The only
escape is annihilation. Man must destroy his will to live
so as to destroy the illusion of thinking, the illusion of
being.

Five years after Hegel's death, Marx, the young off-
spring of a long line of Jewish rabbis, went to that university and absorbed the teaching of Hegel's followers.
Marx however entertained a healthy disdain towards
any far-flung theorising. The political conclusions of
Hegelianism, with its religious veneration for the State,
repelled him. His aim was to strike a blow for the man of
flesh and blood, and against the abstract citizen of the
Hegelian State. On the other hand even Marx's concrete
individual is submitted to external forces. He is nothing
but the result of a dialectical process due not to the Idea
but to the development of productive forces. Man is only
the process of his life, and this process is the result of his
material conditions as determined by the dialectical conflict between social classes.

The optimist and the pessimist, the idealist and the
materialist agreed in denying any meaning to man's
awareness of himself. No answer was given to man's
desperate queries: What am I? What do I mean? What
is the sense of my own existence as distinct from the un-
differentiated being of the universe, of the Idea, of the
Will, of a certain class and a certain stage in history?

Strangely enough, the failure of 19th century thinkers
to take into account this most important because most
personal problem of every thinking man, was due precisely to the importance attributed by Descartes, two
centuries before, to man as an individual thinking being.

Hegel's, Schopenhauer's, Marx's disregard of man's individuality was a direct fruit of Descartes' assertion that one's own consciousness of oneself is truth paramount and the basis of all existence. 'I think, I am conscious of my own thinking, and therefore I am.' This was the first, the only directly known reality—myself in my subjective awareness of my own thinking.

Kant proved that Descartes' 'self' had no self-contained reality. I am aware of my own thinking only when I think of something else. A pure awareness of myself and of nothing else does not exist. There is only thought as mere activity (and not as the activity of a soul subsisting by itself), and this rational activity is the basis of all possible existence.

Fichte tried to save man's individuality by considering man as an individual will—but man's self-awareness, even according to Fichte, was only a case (a special and limited case) of a universal self-awareness which is ultimate reality, an Absolute Self without any limitation. This Absolute, being unlimited, cannot be individual as a 'self' is, and therefore cannot be aware of itself. Hence Hegel maintained that the Absolute is neither consciousness nor something of which thought is conscious. Being is mere rationality, without any distinction between what knows and what is known. As was said above, Hegel called this absolute rationality 'Idea' and proceeded to describe how from its dialectical development everything emerges, both the world and the self. Descartes' one-sided affirmation of the absolute subjectivity of man as a thinking being had produced by logical necessity Hegel's direct negation of man as a self-sufficient reality. Self, God, the world were overwhelmed by the pitiless dialectical course of the Idea. No anthropology, no description of man as he is in himself, as an individual being, was possible.

A revulsion was due. Man as a responsible, self-contained being, man as he had been studied by ancient and mediaeval scholars was bound to re-assert himself. But the spiritual climate of the 19th century was unfavourable. Philosophers were infected either by subjectivism or by historicism. No European thinker was independent enough to take up again the broken thread of anthropology where Descartes' paradox had cut it by disconnecting man's reason and man's body, man and God, man and the world.

It is indeed difficult for the learned to disentangle themselves from the intellectual fashion of their times. To be able to live, they have to get a job—often a teaching job. They have to find publishers and readers. Their teachers, their colleagues, their critics, their public have already their 'own' opinions—which being the opinions of cultured men, are mostly the opinions of teachers they have listened to, or other writers they have read. Thinkers and writers out of fashion are studied only as a matter of erudition, as material for exercises in historical research and literary interpretation. When one's opinions are not the opinions prevailing in the cultured sets of the time, one may be a genius, but this does not enable one to reach the ear of one's contemporaries. A creative engineer may find a new gadget, and if it is good and useful, it will be adopted. A self-made businessman may capture a market, and become an economic power. An independent poet, a thinker without contemporary affiliations falls at once into some forgotten corner of libraries and second-hand bookshops—and remains there till some later scholar discovers him and takes him up again as a subject of scholarly research. Then and only then will an independent thinker be able to exert his influence on the culture of another age.

Therefore a revolt against 19th century impersonal philosophies could occur only in the spirit of some individual who remained alone in his ivory-tower, and in his desolate loneliness could be able to turn his undivided

attention upon himself and live his life with a full awareness, so as to see its meaning and to understand himself.
Nobody of course can reach the bedrock of himself, but
some privileged individual can understand himself better
than the usual run of mankind, and discover some definite meaning in human existence. Sœren Kierkegaard
(1813-1855) was the first 'existentialist', or rather the
first thinker of modern times who reinstated the point
of view of pre-modern anthropology.

To explain his thought one has to speak of his life, for
this was the fundamental set of facts which he had to
interpret in order to build up his theory of man. His life
was uneventful. He was born sickly, in a strongly religious family. His studies were rather desultory. He
became betrothed but this was broken off after a few
months. On the other hand, he liked the good things of
life and lived too expensively. His many writings are
clear when read one by one but their overall meaning
cannot be understood so easily because in each book
Kierkegaard looked at human existence from a different
standpoint according to his own changing moods. His
life was commonplace, so much so that his broken engage-
ment is practically the greatest mystery and tragedy of
his life. Nevertheless, his very normal experiences gave
importance and depth to his conceptions, due neither to
the impact upon his soul of clamorous events nor of dis-
turbing tragedies. What he felt as a tragedy, what he
deemed important and a fit subject for meditation, was
the everyday life of everybody. Kierkegaard's adventure
and tragedy were created by his spiritual insight which
enabled him to peer into the depths of everyday happenings.

According to some reports, a strange episode would
explain the sense of doom which haunted his mind. It
seems that his father as a boy had tended sheep on the
moors of Jutland, freezing in winter, burnt in summer.
His life was so miserable that once he climbed upon a hill

and shaking his small fists at the sky, cursed God who allowed a child to suffer so much. He repented of it when he had grown up and was in better circumstances, but the recollection of his sin overshadowed his soul. He even believed that many of his children had died young owing to God's vengeance. Possibly Kierkegaard derived from his father an acute feeling of the omnipresence of a vengeful God. His father had sinned and brought God's ire on his children—every man alive has to expiate Adam's sin and therefore human life is always bitter and grey even when God's power does not reveal itself openly by some tragical event.

The Calvinistic outlook of his father, his own sickly constitution, his introvert attitude forbade him to accept the ponderous and safe optimism of his church and of his Hegelian teachers at the university of Copenhagen. He was meant by his father for the ministry (like his brother who became a bishop) and theology was his first interest, but neither the Hegelian theology of Marheineke nor the anti-Hegelian sentimental religiosity of Schleiermacher could influence his religious experience. Neither could he follow the path of Feuerbach and Strauss, and accept an identification of God with the Absolute and of the Absolute with historical mankind. Kierkegaard's God, omnipresent in human life, could not be conjured away by historical or idealistic incantations. Kierkegaard was the first fundamentalist in an epoch of positivism and agnosticism and (what was worse) of rational and reasonable Christianity. Revelation stood before him, massive, unbreakable. Like Kafka's hero he felt himself to be on trial for his soul's life.

Hegelian and marxist philosophies resulted from a belief in the dialectical development of history. No opposition, no contrast is definitive. Against every 'Yes' there is always a 'No', but only for a time. Both 'Yes' and 'No' are at last blended and conciliated and 'superseded' by a synthesis, by a higher 'Yes-No'. Every struggle, every disso-

nance, every difficulty is bound to disappear. Kierkegaard's experience of his own existence taught him
instead that no conflict, no inconsistency of human existence can ever be solved. Existence is contradictory in
itself. It is an inescapable 'Either-Or'. So that, for instance, Kierkegaard himself, personally, was not guilty,
and yet he stood condemned, personally, for his father's
sin. Each of us feels personally responsible for his own
acts and for them alone; nevertheless each one of us is
under sentence for Adam's sin and is guilty by the very
fact that he is alive. He is guilty of being a man. No dialectical absolution is possible. If a man refuses God's judgment, he is an existence (i.e. a limited being) no more—
he may overcome his limitations, but he loses his human
individuality. If he escapes responsibility, he loses himself deeper still because he is human no longer. He is like
a stone or an animal.

Moral conscience is in itself contradictory. To escape
inherited guilt one should be able to assert one's own
absolute freedom. But freedom implies responsibility,
and this means that one's every action will be imputed to
him as a sin and a crime. Or rather, as freedom and
responsibility are the very core of human existence, one's
being oneself and nobody else is anxiety. Were man not
anxious about himself, he would not *be*. Sometimes man
is tempted to give up freedom and moral personality, and
to find pause in a heavy resignation to his own guilt. But
this means utter annihilation of the individual. It is the
'mortal disease'. It is desperation, the ultimate crime
against oneself, the sin against the Holy Ghost. When a
man is sick unto this ultimate death he is not really resigned to God's judgment. He has only given up his own
existence, and is lost without redemption.

There seems to be an escape from existential anxiety.
One may shove moral conscience aside and live one's own
life on a lower plane, taking up what Kierkegaard calls
the 'aesthetic' position, i.e. the position of a man who

lives only by his senses, and considers beauty as an ultimate value; but even in this situation existence is not
peace and safety. One is doomed still. Aesthetic contentment is a passing mood, and it is not possible to relax and
enjoy the beauty and the sensual pleasure won. Although
one struggled and fought, yet when the aim has been
attained, enjoyment surfeits at once. Victory bores.
To escape boredom one has to begin struggling again for
something else. The doom of aesthetic existence was
described by Kierkegaard in one of his best books, the
*Diary of a Seducer.* For a long time the seducer plans
and works to debauch Cordelia. But the first night of
love is scarcely passed, and there is no more desire
because there is a struggle no more. There remains
only habit and dreariness. The seducer escapes in the
morning and does not even look back at the girl of his
love.

Such is Kierkegaard's conception of human existence,
his 'existentialism'. Of course, this is only a rationalised
travesty of his teaching. Kierkegaard himself did not, and
could not, expound it as a rational system, as a structure of
theoretical truths. The nature of existence is paradoxical
and therefore it cannot be explained in a consistent sequence
of logical statements. The only proper description of existence is to live it through. Each writing of Kierkegaard
is a partial description, an endeavour to understand the
meaning of some feelings and moods, of some existential
'situation'. But no single situation is existence in the
absolute. Existence is contradictory and casual. If you
stop and build up a logical overall explanation, individual
existence evaporates in generalities. Existentialism must
be at the same time a personal confession, and an interpretation valid for everybody. This is the real difficulty
of a theory of human existence. One has, indeed, to read
all Kierkegaard's writings, each one of them contradicting
or contrasting with the other, each one describing only
one side, either the aesthetical or the moral or the reli-

gious side of existence. It is not possible to connect them together in a rational whole. One can only perceive some kind of general meaning.

This new method—or rather this lack of method—in a speculative exposition is strange when compared with run-of-the-mill philosophical treatises. But it does not lack precedent. In many other cases thinkers, instead of presenting only the result of their research, tried to present the slow and always partial revelation of truth as it dawned upon them, and blended together personal confession and general statements. Their writings too implied existentialism of a kind. They were indeed studies of man because they described general being as known through and by a certain living man.

A good model of existential exposition can be found in many dialogues by Plato which do not conclude with a definite statement. The interlocutors maintain personal opinions and represent a set of different existential positions in regard to the problem in hand. Their discussion does not end in a logical conclusion because the debate itself and the clash of personal opinions (as against scientific truth) proves indirectly Plato's main principle, the paramount value of reason in human existence.—In his *Confessions* St. Augustine lived again his own life against the background of God's omnipresence. Meditation on his own pettiest doings (a childish theft of pears, for instance) allowed him to build up a coherent interpretation of his own existence when confronted with eternal truths. Through this existential consciousness St. Augustine reached an insight into ultimate realities: time and eternity, God's creation, etc.—Even Descartes' first philosophical work, the *Discourse on Method*, starts from a personal account of his own education and doubts.

Existential methods and expositions are not literature, but must have artistic quality. Kierkegaard was a great writer, as were Plato and St. Augustine. Otherwise Kierkegaard would never have been able to present the

H

groundwork of his ideas (his own experience, his own feelings and hopes and fears) so as to make us realise they are also our own experience, our own feelings. Man's life is repetition, endless and dreary iteration. Any one of our days is only a day like another. The tree and the woman painted by Leonardo are just a tree and a woman like many others, but the skill of the artist gives them relevance. Only when our everydays become relevant have they an existential, i.e. a human meaning.

The problem of the philosophic or theoretical value of existential descriptions is more involved. Kierkegaard's experiences were his own experiences, they represented his point of view about himself. Was he justified in giving to individual facts the significance of a general description of human existence? By stressing both his personal experience, and human bondage to paradoxical inconsistencies, he deliberately jettisoned rationality which is coherence and universality. Was he then right in drawing general conclusions from disconnected facts?

What kept everything together, what made Kierkegaard's own experience and his existential interpretation understandable and significant, was faith. Without God and God's judgment, no meaning could be seen in human existence. Man passes like a shadow, *is* a shadow, but a shadow of the Infinite. Should we consider him as an absolute being in his own limited existence, anxiety and desperation would be only mental distempers. They would have no meaning. They have one when they are seen as basic qualities of man's situation as against the Almighty.

Therefore Kierkegaard's human experience had a depth beyond his own individuality. He saw himself as at a distance—the distance of man from God. Aesthetic experience was unsatisfactory, for there was another human position—moral conscience. The moral position was again contradictory as there was yet another cycle of exis-

tence—religious existence, man as beneath God. Therefore Kierkegaard's existential experience was not, let us
say, 'flat'. It had relief and depth, a third dimension,
because it was lived against the background of Kierkegaard's infinite distance from God. It was not indeed a
*philosophy* of existence, i.e. a system of general statements spun out of Kierkegaard's isolated personality.
This would have been absurd. It was rather a contem-
plation of his own humanity which presupposed God and
implied eternity. It was indeed a *theology* of existence—
and only from the standpoint of theology can existentialism be regarded as a consistent and rational point of view.

When existentialism forgets God and tries to build on
mere personal experience a theory of the human being,
when it tries to elicit from the experience of the lonely
individual some general aspect which might reveal the
intimate nature of existence, it is neither philosophy nor
theology. It is a meaningless literary exercise. This happened with Nietzsche, who may well be considered as the
only 'existentialist' in the stretch of time between Kierkegaard and contemporary existentialism.

Nietzsche was an artist, so much so that the high
literary quality of his writings made men of letters think
he was a great philosopher. Half-illiterate politicians of
totalitarian persuasion enhanced his fame by using his
brilliant aphorisms as a prop to their meagre spiritual
goods.

Nietzsche's thought and works are nonetheless bundles
of contradictions. Karl Jaspers had an easy task to prove
that only by considering Nietzsche as an existentialist
could he be made to mean something. Indeed Nietzsche's
'superman' is a very superficial conception derived from
primitive ideas on biological evolution—a kind of abstract
image of what man will be in the next stage of his
development.

The superman is in some way an understudy of discarded Divinity. Human existence must indeed be compared, 'fixed' as against something greater and better, in order to be seen in its forlornness and imperfection, in its petty tragedy. According to Kierkegaard the background of existence was God, i.e. something *beyond* man. Not only was existence an insufficient kind of being: it was insufficient in its ability to account for itself. By proclaiming that 'God is dead' Nietzsche was forced to find his standard of comparison in human existence itself, to explain the limits of man by his very humanity. The superman is only man tomorrow. Man in this more exalted state is the counterpart and standard on which to judge of the lowliness of his actual existence.

Nietzsche's atheism was postulated by his existentialism. He thought that existence as it is in itself could be 'explained' only if one does away with God. Nevertheless this gave a new lease of life to the old impersonalism of Hegel. If existence indeed can be understood only by comparing it to the existence of tomorrow, if only the superman gives meaning to man, man is a creature of time, and the very conception of existence depends on evolution or biological progress. Man's history comes before man's existence, and this implies that there is something beyond existence—there is history, evolution, progress. Existence, again, does not stand alone. It is absorbed and dissolved as a transient moment of an impersonal flow of becoming.

Neither Kierkegard nor Nietzsche were the fathers of contemporary existentialism. This was originated by a quite different line of thought—by Husserl's phenomenological method.

Edmund Husserl was certainly the most distinctive thinker of the first half of the 20th century. It is scarcely possible to give in a few words an inkling of his conceptions. He was originally a mathematician and a logician. His logical researches brought him to face the problem of the elements of logic.—What are the ideas or conceptions about which valid statements can be made? Our awareness of mental contents precedes our judging and reasoning. To elicit what they are, what it is that we reason about, one must find which are our fundamental intuitions in their isolated nakedness.

In our thinking we instinctively confuse the 'essence' or proper significance of what we think and speak about, and our judgment on its correspondence with reality— our knowledge that this or that mental content is, or is not, 'objective'. Only by 'suspending' any judgment about the reality of a mental content (this is the 'phenomenological reduction') will one be able to reach the bedrock of our real knowledge—the 'essences' which correspond to basic acts of our thinking and have a universal validity because thought starts from and builds up on these intuitions. Essences, and essences only, are the building material of all logical structures, of any reasoning and thinking whatsoever.

The phenomenological method used by Husserl to elicit the true contents of our 'intuition of essences' is relevant to the present subject only because it implies that both psychology and history are not scientifically sound. If indeed our reasoning is universally valid, the subject-matter of our reasoning (the essences) cannot change. They are necessary and permanent. They are independent of individual peculiarities, as are logical structures. On the contrary psychology considers our intuitions as due to mental processes, as a product of mental activity influenced by changing external and physiological causes. History on the other hand would have essences changing with the evolution of mankind. Nothing could then be known positively. History according to Husserl brings scepticism in its wake, it is nothing else but scepticism about our knowing.

Many philosophers between 1913 and 1925 came to use, in widely different fields of research, phenomeno-

logical methods even when they started from other philosophical assumptions. Scheler tried to apply phenomenology to our emotional life so as to elicit essential moral
values from a phenomenological analysis of our moral
conscience. He was not exactly an existentialist but came
very near to a phenomenological conception of human
existence. Had he lived longer he would probably have
evolved a phenomenological existentialism as Heidegger
did a little before Scheler's death.

To explain properly the meaning of Heidegger's theory
one may begin by considering the phenomenological
standpoint in regard to time. Essences and logic are not
temporal, are above and beyond time. Their universality
and necessity imply that they are somehow independent
of the temporal flow of our consciousness. But what is
time if it has nothing to do with the fundamental elements of our knowing? Why does our mind think 'in
time'? Why do our intuitions and our reasoning 'happen'?
Husserl had tried to explore the nature of time by using
the phenomenological reduction of it. Time appears as
the *continuum* (the 'place') in which everyone is aware of
essences. Therefore the nature of time and the nature
of the individual (i.e. of our awareness of ourselves as
individual beings, as 'selves') are connected.

Phenomenological reduction implies that it is possible
for us to distinguish between existence and essence, i.e.
*to be* as against *to be thought of* as a certain permanent
intuition. This distinction is due to different acts of individual knowing, and acts of individual knowing are
distinct as different points in the stream of consciousness.
If essences are beyond time and one can reach them only
by avoiding thinking about being, this means that being,
time and individual thought are connected in such a way
that the innermost-nature of being (as distinct from logical essences, from our intuitions) may be discovered by a
phenomenological analysis of our very existence.

This is a very superficial and far from satisfactory re-
construction to explain how phenomenology and existentialism came to be related in Heidegger's mind when he
wrote *Being and Time*, a work which has exercised great
influence on European thought although it has been left
somehow in the air by its author. Heidegger indeed published only the first half of his work, that which contains a
phenomenological description of existence. But the overall aim of his undertaking was *being* in general, i.e.
metaphysics, to be dealt with in a second part by applying
to the analysis of being the results of his existential research. One can say in a way that Heidegger is considered
the greatest contemporary existentialist only because he
failed to complete the task he had undertaken. His initial
assumption was that existence was the proper approach
to the problem of being in general because human existence, i.e. individual man, is a 'privileged case' of being.
Man indeed *is* because he *knows* being. His knowing
constitutes his being: 'the comprehension of being is the
determination of the being of existence.' Knowing, on
the other hand, is aware of itself, so that in man, and in
man alone, being 'enlightens itself', becomes 'transparent
unto itself'. These statements gave a metaphysical standing to existentialism, to the description of human
existence.

One can overlook the failure of Heidegger to live up to
his undertaking. One can forget that existentialism was
justified only as an introduction to metaphysics. But how
could Heidegger justify his existentialism, his research
into the nature of man starting from *phenomenological*
assumptions? Phenomenological methods imply an elimination of being to find out essences or basic intuitions
as they are before any statement about their reality is
made. How can one apply phenomenological methods to
the description of the *being* of man?

Here lies the originality of Heidegger. *Ex-istere* (in
German, *Da-sein*) means literally 'to be there', i.e. to be

in a certain point and not elsewhere. Heidegger thought
that by 'suspending' the 'to be' and examining the 'there'
he would be able to analyse the essence of existence as
distinct from its being. Now, one might think that very
little may be elicited from the simple word 'there'. Yet
'there' implies that every position of existence, every
actual condition of man is not essentially different from
any other. Man simply is 'there'. No one 'there' is higher
than another 'there'. Man's consciousness of himself results from the most common, usual words he uses about
himself. Philological interpretation ('hermeneutic') of
such usual expressions will allow us to understand the
essence of existence. Now the most common signification
given to 'there' is 'being in the world'. Heidegger goes
on to interpret first 'world', then 'being in', then 'in'.
Moreover, 'being in the world' implies 'being together',
and the hermeneutic of 'together' reveals that there are
other nondescript existences, that there are other 'ones'
besides ourselves.

At this point Heidegger takes up Kierkegaard's results
but gives to them a twist which is the seed of contemporary existentialism. 'Being in the world', 'being together' mean that man is perpetually in danger of losing
himself in the world and among the nondescript 'ones'
with whom he exists. Therefore the fundamental attitude
of existence is an attitude of anxiety. Heidegger however
cannot take account of God or moral values because his
phenomenological standpoint forbids him to presuppose
any being. Hermeneutic of being cannot lean on anything else but existence. Our anxiety results immediately
from the very fact that existence means 'being in the
world', but anxiety in regard to the world is something
definite, different today and tomorrow, different in one
and in another 'there': it is anxiety about something. It
is not an original attribute of our own existence, an
'existential'. The real essence of anxiety depends upon
the quality of our existence in general, from the 'there'

without a particular object—one can say, from an attitude (an 'existential') towards ourselves and not towards the world. This vague, permanent and steady trouble about ourselves is not anxiety but uneasiness, preoccupation, 'worry'. We are worried. Existence is worry because we feel perpetually on the verge of losing ourselves in the world or in the grey mass of nondescript 'ones' with whom we are together. Existence is being worried about itself, is (roughly) a fear of losing itself in a nondescript something from which it has to save itself on every side. Thus worry produces succession and time: 'existence temporalizes itself.' Time therefore is the 'place' in which existence exists. Man is a historical being, lives in history, his world is history. In this way, by reversing Husserl's analysis of time, Heidegger denied the fundamental assumption of Husserl that history is a scepticism which makes any research, any logical statement void and meaningless.

At this point a bridge to metaphysics should be found. *Being and Time* ends indeed:

Now, how is a revealing understanding of being possible according to (the nature of) existence? Can we answer by referring to the ontological structure (which is time) of existence as a being which understands being? How can we interpret this temporalizing of temporality? Is there a way from original time (i.e. time due to existential worry) to the meaning of being? Does time reveal itself as the horizon of being?

As was remarked above, Heidegger stopped here although an analysis of existence left in the air, without a subsequent theory of being, made absurd the very reason given at the beginning for analysing existence—that existence is a privileged case of being. Moreover, whilst the study of being is not completed, existence remains without meaning. The 'hermeneutic' method of Heidegger was meant indeed to discover the essence of being starting from that peculiar being which is existence.

*Being and Time* is not a phenomenological analysis aiming only at discovering the essence of existence. It was meant as a potential metaphysics. Incomplete as it is, *Being and Time* is pure hermeneutic, not an existentialism: it describes what 'human existence' *means*, not what human existence *is*.

Nevertheless this incomplete metaphysics miscalled 'existentialism' conjured up, as soon as it was published, one of those strange storms that so often sweep the intelligentsia off their feet. Such fashions give an unnatural twist to cultural interests, and alter the proper balance of a consistent cultural world by giving an undue relevance to a particular kind of research and to some one-sided theory. Especially in Germany is such an occurrence dangerous since that is the European country most interested and most competent in philosophical questions. The Hegelian cult which arose in Germany in the first half of the 19th century influenced the structure of European civilization by way of an undue optimism about the destiny of mankind. So, a century later, pessimism and philosophy of history were spread abroad by the publication of Spengler's *Decline of the West*, because a representative of Germany, which had been defeated in World War I, was inclined to think that the whole of Europe was foundering with her and that the end of Western civilization was impending. The foolish optimism about Progress and Evolution, which for two centuries had given to the European intelligentsia sound sleep and happy dreams, was challenged. Public opinion retained the optimism it had been taught, but the intelligentsia, made slightly wiser by blood and fear and the despondency of an uneasy peace, began to realize that European civilization might fail and disappear. Spengler's theories were eagerly discussed. A number of proposals and quack remedies for Europe's revival and disinfestation were brought forth—with the results, or

the lack of results, we have lately experienced in World
War II and after.

Almost on the heels of the Spengler vogue (nine years
later) Heidegger's existential pessimism gave renewed expression to the despondency of Germany. Germans were
inclined to believe that anything would be better than
freedom. Communism and Nazism loomed on the horizon. The Weimar republic was on the rocks. Heidegger's
message was ideally suited for a crowd of learned men who
found it easier to lament and wring their hands over the
corruption of the times than to use their hands and wits
to some useful purpose. Heidegger became popular because his theories offered a common ground to all popular
'isms'. Every kind of thinker could indeed accept, and
distort further, Heidegger's conceptions. Existentialism
could be accepted by the vitalist who believed that life is
everything and that reason is only a set of meaningless
tricks. Truth and sanity can be found in life itself, life
unimpeded by moral or rational schemes, life naked and
unashamed. James, Bergson, Croce, the last followers of
Nietzsche were all vitalists in their own way, and now
their followers found in Heidegger a new prophet.

The historicist too found a congenial atmosphere in the
school of existentialism which, although it started from
a theory which was opposed on principle to historicism,
had ended by justifying and praising history. Misch,
son-in-law, heir and literary executor of Dilthey, the
most celebrated historicist and vitalist of the times, tried
to keep his feet on firm ground by maintaining that
Dilthey's historicism could never be attuned to phenomenological methods and existentialism. He nevertheless stressed many similarities between Heidegger and
Dilthey, so that the real difference between them was no
longer seen.

Anybody who was able to clothe his own philosophy in
an existentialist garb could indeed share in Heidegger's
popularity. A few first-rate thinkers like Jaspers (who

tried to save the rational character of existence) and
Berdyaev (in a peculiar way) gave a sort of coherence to
Heidegger's existentialism. But the vogue of existentialism could not last long in Germany. Skilled thinkers
as they are, German philosophers soon worked the existentialist poison out of their system. The very fact that
Heidegger himself had found it impossible to complete
his work, proved to them that existentialism was a philosophy for the amateur. Yet men of letters all over
Europe were seduced by the opportunity offered for fanciful juggling with mystical words like 'situation', 'worry',
'boredom', 'horizon', etc. As a justification of all bad habits
of thought which are prevalent in contemporary Europe
(historicism, vitalism, irrationalism, etc.) existentialism
preserves even today a certain appeal for countries less
skilled in philosophy than Germany.

An existentialist epidemic broke out in Italy when
Heidegger's influence was already on the wane in Germany, before World War II. During the war and immediately after it the vogue went further. In France the
fashion spread far and wide, harmoniously blending
existentialism, bohemian life, communism, homosexual-
ity, the cafés and the theatre. Radical pessimism and
uncompromising atheism made existentialism the proper
faith of anybody who wished to justify Russian marxism,
left-wing Labour, and the 'new masses'. Heidegger
taught indeed that existence is 'being together' and this
may be made to mean that existence is a result of nondescript mankind, that man can be understood only as an
atom in an amorphous mass.

Christian 'democracy' and the Churches could not allow
the Marxists alone to make propaganda out of the existentialist vogue. The existentialist field came to be split
between a religious and an atheistic denomination, a
natural schism due to the mongrel quality of contemporary
existentialism, born in the bosom of Christian faith and
then given over to the good offices of the devil. As a

matter of fact, the last wave of existentialism which later on swept over Britain and America, is now receding. It seems scarcely worth while to discuss it, were it not that every disappearing fashion leaves some scattered ideas (usually, the worst ones) incrusted in the mind of the amateur and the man of letters who know little about other and more serious philosophies. After-effects of the existentialist vogue have given a new lease of life to many 'isms' which contribute to the present decay of European culture and morals—to marxism, to historicism, to idealism, to fascism, to vitalism, to pragmatism. They had already run their course but now are re-incarnated in an existentialist disguise. This current menace to rational, earnest thought, to morality and religion in the cultured classes would not be a valid argument in and by itself. But existentialism or existentialist principles are dangerous just because existentialism is unsound. It is worth while to state again why no existentialism can be considered as a plausible, reasonable doctrine.

Criticism can be based on the fundamental twist undergone by existentialism when it was transplanted from Germany to France. Heidegger's and Jasper's philosophy was basically monistic. Existence, and existence only, was taken into consideration when they tried to describe it. Other forms of being were only 'positions' of existence, just as according to Hegel every form of being was only a 'position' of the Idea. The hermeneutic analysis of the *Da* of the *Dasein* discovered in existence itself the ground of 'being in a world' and of 'being together'. In other words, different forms of being were in a sense produced by existence's searching and peering all round itself (Jasper's *Umgreifendes*). A strong idealistic, Hegelian flavour permeated German existentialism.

Sartre's *L'être et le néant* on the other hand shows the influence of Descartes' dualism. Man is radically different from '*les choses*'. The doom of existence, anguish, is not due to an internal quality of existence itself but to man being confronted by 'things' and obliged to take a position as against them. Only in this sense could Sartre make existentialism equivalent to humanism, i.e. to the effort of producing man, instead of taking existence as a datum which cannot possibly evolve into something else.

This was certainly what Sartre meant. The very word 'humanism' refers to the Renaissance and its assumption that man had to be developed, brought to perfection by a greater consciousness of his own nature. Existentialist humanism tends instead to debase mankind. 'Things' produce within existence a reaction which makes man responsible without giving him dignity and moral power. These considerations prove again that existentialism, properly speaking, is no self-sufficient philosophy. It is only an anthropology, a theory of man, and an anthropology supposedly able to stand by itself and not, like ancient and Christian anthropology, to be a constituent part of a full-fledged, complete moral and theological system. The fundamental claim of existentialism is that anthropology is the paramount science. Contemporary existentialism cannot therefore appeal to any knowledge or reality superior to man himself. It is knowledge of man and of man alone, denying him even his rationality because reason is universal, is a rule and a law, and therefore beyond mere individuality. Only Jaspers tried to save reason, but perhaps because of this, and of his sound philosophical methods, he failed to exert so deep an influence as did Heidegger and Sartre.

Existentialism by its denial of rationality loses any right to be considered as a coherent system of ideas. Truth and falsehood imply comparison, or reference to some rule. If the ultimate standard of truth is one's own conception of oneself in one's own individuality, nothing one thinks and says can possibly be either true or false since it cannot be judged by general standards. It is true that many others can think and say about themselves what one

thinks and says about oneself: but this is an argument
against existentialism. If indeed I and others can compare
our personal points of view, this means that I can communicate my own conception by words and discourse,
and discourse is a logical context, valid for everybody.
Otherwise I would never be able to make another man
understand what I think when I say, for instance, 'worry'
or 'personal situation'.

If indeed communication is possible and valid, then
man is not an isolated being. The idea of existence is not
closed up into the restricted limits of a single individual.
Any existential description implies something else besides
mere individuality. And existentialism is wrong in asser-
ting that man can be analysed without implying anything
besides man's own individual conception of himself.
Given this solipsistic point of view, 'being together' (i.e.
the actual reality of other existences) is only a figment
arising in the charmed and closed circle of an individual
man.

Even before Heidegger, the theorist of historical methods had run into the difficulty of explaining how an
individual man may be known by another man. If the
task of the historian is to describe men and times in their
distinctive individuality, he should be able to understand
them in their intimate nature, 'to live' them again along
with his own life. If any historical fact is an individual
event and the man who left his historical trace (a book,
an action, etc.) was a real individual being, any historical
fact needs to be 'understood', not only known. It may be
known, of course, by our rational thought, but knowing
gives only generalities. To understand historical individualities one needs another kind of knowledge, a new
faculty which is nowadays termed technically *Verstehen*
as against *Verstand* ('comprehension' as against 'understanding').

Historians (Dilthey for instance) were compelled to

attempt the solution of this problem which arose from their presupposition that history deals with real individualities and not with more or less arbitrary abstractions due to a rational procedure of our mind, as was contended in Chapter I. To explain how we could 'comprehend' individuals they had recourse to analogy, to similarity of feeling, to many other non-rational sides of our mind. They could not escape the obvious fact that if something I say can be 'comprehended' by another man, there must be something in my expression which is not absolutely individual, and therefore that my historical 'comprehension' of an individual is due to something above and beyond the individual, i.e. to something general and rational.

Heidegger believed that he had found a way to explain communication from individual to individual. If existence means 'being together', existence itself implies being in communication with other similar beings, which yet are not clear-cut individualities but nondescript 'ones' vaguely similar to us. Reason therefore would not be necessary to explain communication. The intimate nature of existence is reflected immediately in the words used to express it, so much so that (as was seen above) an analysis of the expression (a 'hermeneutic') is equivalent to an analysis of existence. How and why, he did not say. Jaspers drew from the very fact of communication the conclusion that existence implies a 'casting around' itself. This 'casting around', this extension of one's individuality, means rational expression.

It is clear that the 'one' we actually know or 'comprehend' is either an existence, an individual, self-subsistent being, or it is something (say, the human condition, a human quality) which is common to all possible existences. In the first case, how can I who am aware only of my isolated existence, 'communicate' with, and 'comprehend', another individual existence? In the second case, 'existence' is not an individual but a general conception.

Both the existentialist and the historicist are indeed unable to prove that in this world of mine another existence like myself exists. Only by admitting that my thought includes a general element as well as an awareness of myself as an individual being, can it be assumed that another individual being similar to myself is a man like I am. Another individual is an individual because he is a personality and is a responsible moral being. No such moral individuality can be admitted by the existentialist who holds that freedom and moral law are not native to existence, that existence is bondage to a world, and moral law is outside the scope of existence because it implies something (a rule) beyond and above my individuality.

Sartre tried to evade the issue by supposing that responsibility arose under the impact of external 'things', by our effort to give them significance. Existence is a response, it is not self-sufficient and original. '*Les choses*' are the real basis of man's individuality. But they are beyond existence, they 'transcend' man: therefore Sartre's theory recognized the need of a transcendent being to make 'comprehension' of my own and others' individuality possible. This transcendent being, '*les choses*', is an inferior kind of being. Even so, Sartre comes to confirm the point made by Kierkegaard and forgotten by later existentialists. Kierkegaard indeed understood that we are 'anxious' only because we fail to conform to something greater than ourselves. Heidegger, degrading anxiety to worry, denied to existence any moral quality and abolished the personality of existence. Kierkegaard's anxiety instead did not imply fear only of ceasing to be, fear 'to fall through' being, but also fear of not being as we should be.

A non-theological existentialism should be able to do without any being beyond existence, without this transcendent reality which (as Heidegger himself stated in one of his earlier works) is the absolute object since it is the most general being. By limiting the task of philosophy

I

to the description of existence and nothing else, the existentialist implies that my particular existence is absolute reality. It is then impossible to assume that there can be another existence like me. One is bound indeed to *deny* that there is or can ever be another existence. Consequently existentialism, in the acceptation of Heidegger and Sartre and their followers, is thoroughgoing solipsism—the statement that I, I alone and nothing else exists. This is absolute scepticism because it denies the possibility of knowing anything beyond the limits of one's individual thought or fancy. Unable to escape solipsism, the existentialist makes a virtue of it, and proudly proclaims that existence, and existence alone, is real and that philosophical research starts and ends with the individual.

To *whom* does he proclaim this final dogma, if he is alone in his 'world', if he is 'together' with beings, but does not know whether they are beings like himself? Possibly his solitary worry seems to him heroic. He feels lonely and exalted,

> Pinnacled dim in the intense inane.

Yet the ideal anarchist of Shelley was not a solipsist. He was heroic because he stood up in solitude against the awful forces of the universe and dared to try and free himself from enormous realities that overshadow existence—

> From chance, and death, and mutability.

He meant indeed to be, and strove to be something better than mere existence. On the contrary existentialist man is closed up in his own little world. He is no hero but rather a small shopkeeper who cannot leave his shop and go out on a spree because his little shop makes of him what he is, a shopkeeper. There is indeed something funny in this kind of man. Like Humpty Dumpty, he sits on a wall and worries about falling into the world. But he cannot even fall.

To excuse the light vein of this observation it might be remembered that very often the existentialist makes fun of existentialism by some such outrageous statement as: 'What interests me is not being in general, nor the world, neither is it man in general, man as a species or a general conception. What interests me is myself, I in my own personal individuality and nobody else.' One cannot but wonder why other 'existences' go on listening to him. Any one of them should be interested rather in himself than in the speaker's personal existence and affairs. A poet may be interesting when he speaks about himself—he speaks *to* you. An individual existence which speaks of itself as the only being worthy of note, is not exactly a captivating display. Anyone else will fail to see why one should make a song and dance about it.

Another puzzling affirmation (one finds it in a recent book by an existentialist of note) is that existentialism is essentially a subjectivism, a theory of subjectivity. But Descartes was already a subjectivist. His philosophy was based on the subjective awareness of the self, but he saw also the untenability of solipsistic subjectivism and tried to evade it by drawing from the statement that 'I am because I think' the consequence that God and other men and the world exist. This was countered by the objection that it is impossible to reach any sort of reality by starting from subjective awareness. As has been stated in Chapter II, modern philosophy tried to develop and improve on Descartes' procedure so as to be able to avoid solipsism whilst still basing reality on the self-consciousness of our own thought. If existentialism is absolute subjectivism, the wheel of modern philosophy has now come full circle. European thinkers have gone back to Descartes' initial point and are not to be budged from it. They maintain that philosophy is a subjective dream and cannot be anything else. Existentialism can be regarded as a *reductio ad absurdum* and an implicit criticism of the starting point of modern philosophy. If existentialism is instead meant in earnest, it is a kind of philosophy which had already been reneged and controverted by Descartes, its originator.

The only alternative open to contemporary existentialism is a choice between atheism and religion, between marxism and Christianity, and a return either to Nietzsche's biological vitalism or to Kierkegaard's anxiety and deathly sickness. A short comparison is sufficient to prove that in both cases the existentialist misunderstands either Kierkegaard or Nietzsche.

The marxist is fundamentally right when he appeals to Heidegger. Already in the first flush of the fashion for Heidegger, German marxists found it possible to develop a dialectical phenomenology and to bring existentialism into full accord with marxist tenets. Today existential marxism seems to hold literally to Marx's words. Marx indeed wrote that you have to take the matter at its roots and the root of man is man himself (*Criticism of Hegel's Philosophy of Law*). Modern existentialism eliminates God to leave to existence its absolute loneliness. But the marxist existentialist forgets that, according to Marx, man and the world were only processes, not fixed elements. Otherwise dialectics, social development, the famous 'revolution' would not mean anything. The marxist deems 'revolution' necessary because if man is dependent on his world and vice versa, then only when he changes that world brusquely can he hope to change himself.

If the existentialist is right in assuming that worry is a fundamental quality inherent to existence, and that time and history flow from this quality, no historical event will ever be able to change existence in its innermost substance. Were it able to do so, time and history would be annihilated. Only one true 'revolution' is possible according to existentialism—the annihilation of existence. No other revolution could ever be a real revolution because it would fail to change man according to marxist hopes.

On the other hand existentialism, with its implicit denial of any transcendent reality, be it morals or God, gives to man an absolute value. There is only myself, and my world is my oyster. But this was just what the anarchist Stirner said, and everybody knows there is no love lost between the anarchist and the marxist. They are at the opposite poles of political thought. Nietzsche's position too was in fact anarchical. Marx was an anarchist only in so far as he admitted a lawless struggle for life between classes, not between individuals. Therefore it can be asked whether anarchism or marxism is the ortho-dox atheistic acceptation of existentialism. They seem to be both plausible, and therefore neither is logically sound. Any interpretation is valid. When one posits that life is the highest value, one is saying just nothing. 'Life' means a lot of things, none of them definite. In stating that existence is worry, one can think either of the income-tax return, or of World War III, or of a toothache, or of one's destiny after death. The existentialist would say that they are only different forms assumed by our basic worry, a way to keep alive, to go on being an exis-tence. In this way, greater and lesser worries would be put on the same level. From the standpoint of existen-tialism it is impossible to make a distinction between different values. Each possible pang—whether of one's conscience or one's bunions—is intimately connected, and connected in the same way, to one's innermost existence.

Neither does a religious existentialism seem logical. How can one assume that existence is absolute reality if one admits a God over and above it? It might be answered that Kierkegaard, the recognized father of existentialism, accepted this conception of existentialism: but, on the contrary, the truth is that contemporary doctrine has reversed and stultified Kierkegaard's existentialism which was a theology and not a philosophy, far less a 'religious philosophy'.

Religious existentialism really starts from the incompleteness, the superficiality, the transitoriness of things as they appear immediately in our existence. From this it means ultimately to reach God. In fact God is already there. Transiency and worry already imply something above us, something steady. Otherwise we would never know our existence as the lack of something. This is just the difference between theology and philosophy, between Kierkegaard and his interpreters. Kierkegaard did not start from even a hypothetical lonely existence. God was present to man from the very beginning of his existential research. Contemporary religious existentialism poses instead as a philosophy because it assumes that no existence of God is already involved in our awareness of the limitations of our existence. In so doing existentialism falls into the same mistake as Descartes, who reasoned in a circle when he tried to build a philosophical system on the obvious truth that the very awareness of imperfection includes already an idea of perfection. If indeed it is maintained that existence is worried about itself and that its own nature is worry and nothing else, worry is still a definite awareness. Therefore one should be able to represent unto oneself calm contentment too, so that our very consciousness of ourselves as worry implies already the representation of another mode of being. One is worried because one is aware at the same time of one's own existence and of a totally different kind of existence which is something beyond one's existence.

Religious existentialism seems to take a leaf from the book of St. Augustine who stated that existence is a perpetual fall from the past into the future. We live in a point only, a 'now' which has neither consistency nor reality. But St. Augustine averred that we are able to perceive the transient quality of our being because our soul can 'extend' itself, by memory and anticipation, into the past and into the future.

In any sound existentialism God should come before man. This theological postulate justified Kierkegaard's research. Man's failure to live on, to 'exist' in one or the other mode of existence (aesthetic, ethical, religious) is due to the isolation of each mode from the other. It is either-or. Man cannot live in all three modes at the same time. Existence is imperfect in each mode of existence because the modes are not blended and unified by a dialectical process. There is a synthesis indeed, from the very beginning, but it is beyond man. It is perfect 'existence' or rather absolute being—full happiness, goodness without responsibility, the eternal rectitude of God.

In the heyday of the Heidegger vogue a modest German divine, Koepp, asked whether we could not take love, Christian love, instead of worry, as the really significant 'existential'. If there is God and we are creatures of his love, we are worried only because we feel we cannot live up to this love. . . . That was perhaps naive, but it was sound theology, at least in so far as it averred that our own anxiety, our own existential trouble should prove, if not the reality, at least the possibility of better things. Existentialism is indeed an excuse for sitting down to lament and let the world go by. No morality is possible. There is no rhyme nor reason in our worry. God is far away. Even religious existentialism takes Him into consideration only to prove that man is a worm, of no use even to make fruitful soil out of carrion.

Existentialism is a bankrupt philosophy which is used to excuse a bankrupt Europe. Europe has destroyed herself and neither has the will nor feels the duty to build up again. Kierkegaard looked further, beyond our miserable, well-deserved unhappiness. His gloomy conception of the human condition had an inherent moral quality. Man's anxiety is dejection before the judgment of God.

Man knows that he is damned—and that he is damned justly. This justice is like a naked sword held against ourselves. To escape utter annihilation, to save ourselves, we have only the sword to take hold of, bruising and cutting our hands. Therefore it is forbidden to despair. We must remain anxious. We must suffer and fear.

The existentialist will not take hold of anything. He refuses anxiety. He is resigned to worry. He has escaped from the bondage of morality in which we can feel only remorse. He has escaped from the sight of God to avoid being under judgment. But existence as mere worry is less than existence. It is animality, and it does not allow us to forget ourselves even if we have already *lost* ourselves in our 'everydays', in the maze of casual, meaningless happenings which make up the life of man.

# CHAPTER V

# MAN'S RIPENESS

> Men must endure
> Their going hence, even as their coming hither;
> Ripeness is all.
>
> *Lear*

ANOTHER DAY has ended and it is dark at last. The room is a desert. A frightful loneliness invades it as soon as the door is closed. And the whiteness of the bed is like a page on which nothing has ever, nothing will ever be written but dashes between the parentheses of our sleep.

You fall into sleep as into a final decision. But nothing is concluded—nothing definite happened during your day. There was only the usual routine of washing and eating, of walking and sitting. Some work, which has not yet been finished. Casual meetings, desultory conversations. Meaningless images arising from the newspaper, from the crazy babbling of the wireless. A bundle of transient events without a definite meaning, a single purpose. Out of all this you cannot make a day. Everyday is not even a day.

Does not one's whole life appear as a long everyday when one recollects the past—a punctuation of separate events, of meaningless doings? You do not ever remember why you did this and that, why you chose to write this book, to marry that woman, to pursue one rather than another calling. You feel dimly that your life should have a shape, a meaning—but you cannot see it. To your very eyes your own life appears without significance, or direction.

And yet—you are a rational being. Your thinking has coherence, unity, conclusiveness. But to your own mind your life appears disconnected and casual. The existentialist tries to prove that this meaningless drifting from one everyday to another, from one act to another is your innermost reality. He denies stability and purpose even to our reason.

But living and thinking are one. If thinking starts from a certain point and concludes with a definite result,

130

even our life must be conclusive. To be conclusive it needs be concluded.

Only when we are dead, when the charmed circle begun with our birth has completely revolved, sealed by that death for which we waited and which we feared the more as our awareness increased—only then can our life reach a significant unity.

But then, we are no more. So long as we live, try as we may to trace the course of our own life, we can see but fitful changes, passing shapes in a fog, because we look at our life from the standpoint of an everyday which to-morrow will be there no more. When we have ceased to love a certain woman, the passion which seemed once the very breath of our life, appears quite different. Any one of our yesterdays is just an everyday—a nondescript bundle of acts and happenings which can mean anything. We pass through our life, and cannot stop to look at it steadfastly.

We recollect only atoms of ourselves. We ask ourselves why we have acted in such and such a way. We cannot find an answer. But there must be an answer—in our character, in our personality. We do not know because our whole consciousness is occupied, at each moment, by our immediate experience. Many decisions must be taken, and every decision is perfectly free, due to our-selves as we are in the transient instant. Yet we are un-able to make our decision coherent with the ideal pattern of disparate acts which is our life as seen *from* our life.

Our biographer will not be a captive of our yesterdays, of the different situations in which we found ourselves when the moment came for decision and action. He can forget our nights and days. He can find in the dreary series of our everydays some relevant event which though perhaps we did not even remark it yet went to make of us what we are—what we are everlastingly when our life is ended and its pattern, the pattern of our personality, is clear:

Tels qu'en *nous* mêmes enfin l'éternité *nous* change.

We saw only isolated decisions. Our biographer, being a man endowed like ourselves with free will, will be able to understand our decisions and to see them as a coherent whole—our character, our personality. Personality will then appear as the intimate, coherent destiny which has ruled our lives.

What then is personality, the character of man, if man is free and his own personality is built up by free acts of his will, and yet his personality is a destiny which binds him in such a way that he could not do but what he did? How can it be said that the biographer can know and describe a man as he was, as a unity, a well-balanced construction—when every man who lives knows himself to be unhampered, free to take any decision, even a decision contrasting with all other decisions he took previously?

A man does not see the meaning of each single decision. The meaning results only from the complete pattern of all his decisions. Yet it is he who decided, and in so doing created his own being. Only his biographer can see the pattern, the meaning. But how can he see it, when he cannot understand the single decision which was known only by the man who was its author? Is biography then only an abstract summary of the life of an individual, scarcely related to his life as it was in its innermost core?

To the biographer indeed, as to anybody else, every action of a man is known only as an external occurrence. Nobody can see the intentions of another individual, can truly *understand* any action of another. The bystander can believe that a selfish action was due to an impulse of benevolence. An act of apparent courage may have been caused by the fear of appearing a coward, or even by an instinctive movement... Yet the biographer, even many years and centuries later, and though knowing about his subject perhaps far less than contemporaries, is able to peer into intentions and recognize them as those of a distinct personality, simply because the life of that individual is ended—concluded as a clause between the capital letter of birth and the full stop of death. A casual death, perhaps—a car smash, a cold taking a bad turn. How can an accidental happening be a conclusion? Why should the full stop come always when the period is closed so that the biographer can read it as a complete statement?

The answer is that the full stop is already implicit in the capital letter at the beginning—man is born to die. In the first wailing of the newly born there is already some mortality. Man progresses from wailing to lisping his first words, from lisping to speaking and so forth. But he can be stopped at any moment, after any word can come the full stop, any word may be the last, and therefore is such that it may be the conclusive word of the clause. Any action might be the last action, and therefore each action is conclusive. Or, each action 'bends' our life in a peculiar curve so that at the end of every life the circle closes.

This is the ultimate meaning of death that comes as a thief in the night. Every action shall be done as if it were our last, without any possibility of repentance or redress. The responsibility of anyone for his several actions means that his life as a whole, wherever death catches up with him, has to be concluded. Each action 'bends' so as to fit into the circle, so as to have a meaning, even if in his acting man takes upon himself the responsibility of that single action only and does not see that he is shaping the pattern of all his actions, and is making himself responsible even for his character and his destiny.

All this does not prove the possibility of biographical knowledge. There remains the clash between the intent of an action (which is unknown to the biographer) and its meaning (which is unknown to the living agent). There remains the problem of personality which is indeed an identity of two contraries—on one hand it is spontaneous growth due to free volition, on the other hand it is a destiny ruling all actions.

This contrast is inherent in any moral action, in any action which is really human, which is due to the decision of a rational being, and not to instinctive, irresponsible, non-deliberate movements.

Reason is necessity. A sensation and a feeling do not imply that everybody else will perceive and feel the same; but rational thinking implies that what we think cannot but be true, and true for everybody. When one perceives, say, a certain sound, one does not think it impossible to perceive a different sound, or not to perceive anything at all. To *feel* seedy does not imply that everybody else must feel seedy. But since I *think* that two times two is four, I cannot think that for anyone else it might be five. When one draws from certain premises a logical consequence, one is certain that any other rational being would draw the same consequence.

Moral acting does not have the accidental aspect of a perception or feeling. Deliberate action implies that any other rational being is bound to act in the same way. Moral acting refers to reason, is endowed with rational necessity and universality. In the very moment I decide that it is my duty to act in a certain way, I fix an absolute rule. My decision implies that I think any other action, in this my personal situation (which in fact cannot happen again, or happen to anyone else) would not be a moral action—would be immoral or non-moral. Every moral action of anybody imports a law, is a judgment on the man who acts and on the rest of mankind.

It is strange indeed that the isolated deliberation and action of a single man may have this universal meaning. Yet it is no more strange than the fact that when one excogitates a new theory, a certain logical sequence, one thinks at the same time both that it cannot be otherwise, and that it must be valid for everybody, even if nobody else ever thought of it before.

Reason indeed is a law unto itself—reason is reasoning and the law of reasoning. And in the same way, moral acting is moral law-giving. Therefore no deliberate action is an isolated event. It is both an action and the statement of a moral principle. It implies a similar acting on the part of everybody. And as in the domain of reason each several truth is necessarily connected with every other truth, a moral action conditions every moral action of any kind whatsoever. If today we have thought it right to help a blind man across the street, tomorrow we cannot escape the duty of trying to save somebody who is drowning. In short, by being the action of a rational being, a moral action is constructive. It is not isolated, even if at the moment we do not perceive its implications.

Man's basic peculiarity and strangeness is that his individuality has a universal value. He can think and act because he is conscious of himself as a specific individual who thinks and acts. But just because he is himself and nobody else, his thinking and acting have a general purport and extent. His very individuality (which from the standpoint of his moral, or immoral, acting is called 'his personality') is based on the universality of his reason.

In the same way any decision, just because it is due to an individual as a personality, and to him alone, is absolutely free but is also a freely posited law which binds him irretrievably. The individual is free because he is bound by his own laws. In this way each action conditions all his future actions, and is conditioned by his previous actions, by the laws he has given to himself whenever he acted with the utmost and innermost liberty. The individual may well forget his past actions. Still, they have been done, and laws of his own making exist. If any one of his actions disregards these laws, he is incoherent—incoherent as an individual. He does not have a personality.

Therefore his freedom creates his destiny; and indeed his personality, according to the point of view from which it is considered, is either destiny or freedom. From the standpoint of his several decisions (the standpoint of everybody when he lives his everyday life in which deliberate acting and impulsive or unconscious acts are mixed) the individual is perfectly free. But when one looks at the constructive aspect of any of his moral actions, he is under a law, under the doom of his personality, of his being made such as he is, or better, of his having made himself such as he is.

The behaviourist claims that one's destiny results from one's conditioning, from external events, and not from one's reason, from the core of one's soul. The biologist maintains that a personality is governed by heredity, by physiological peculiarities, as by fate. The marxist states that there is no such thing as a personality and that the behaviour of any man is due to economic conditions, to mass-impulses. They admit destiny and deny freedom. This means that they deny to man his rational quality upon which necessity and universality and destiny depend, and instead give to his destiny an external origin, a non-human cause.

Freedom indeed depends on our rational awareness. A stone let free can but fall down. Man, when he is conscious of his doings, is conscious also of what is forcing him to act in a certain way, and this very consciousness gives him a freedom to resist. When he does not think, he follows the impulse—but not as a rational soul, not as a human being. When he thinks, by the very act of thinking, he is able to resist or to follow—he is free in his will, and guilty if his impulse wins and makes him act like a stone. Consciousness, and in particular moral consciousness, an awareness of freedom and responsibility, is not there always. Man is a rational being by fits and starts. Reasoning is too often only a possibility (and an unfulfilled duty), even though man is man only because he is a rational being.

The child is the result of his heredity, his environment, his body, just because he is not yet, or is only dimly, a rational being. He begins to have clear moments, and these moments are *his* moments. In other moments he is submerged in, and is a part of, his world. Slowly, out of the hard crust of his heredity and of the external conditions of his life, from this nondescript bundle of stuff in the immense world, there emerges a rational being. Once, at least, his consciousness and his impulses may clash. If he decides to resist, the crust is cracked and he can grow up, building his destiny. He becomes a personality. If he decides not to resist, he is another kind of being, one who has resigned his power, and submitted to external destiny—a rational larva in a sealed cocoon.

His biographer will try to peer into the cocoon. He was a man, a reasonable being. . . . But he had used his reason as his body dictated. His life was the existence of a stone, of a tree. It has meaning only as an element in the landscape. He does not stand up as a personality which is a building and a world in itself.

Too often biographies are tedious catalogues of facts, a chronicle of isolated events and actions such as the man himself could have written. They are a diary written by another, an easy task indeed. A superficial biographer has no trouble in the choice of his facts—he has only to collect the events which happened to that individual. He has no trouble in ordering them—he has only to begin from birth and to go on till death. Really, writing such biographies does not imply either greater learning or deeper insight than editing daily news. They are not biographies. They are studies in natural history.

A good biographer should find unity in the life of his man. Unity, personality, destiny—they are the same.

K

It is always a meaning which must be elicited. The sequence of facts and actions is meaningless in and by itself. What is significant is the whole. Mere happenings of a life constitute only a two-dimensional section of a personality which has three dimensions. The meaning does not belong to the sequence of time but to permanence, to a unity above the sequence even if it arose out of the sequence. Death having closed the circle, the biographer can see it from above, as a complete circle, even when he follows and describes its successive points from birth to death.

What is it that gives the biographer this insight? Why is he unable to know the innermost intent of a single action of another man, and yet able to understand the personality which underlies the whole series of the facts and acts of another life?—His capacity derives from the logical coherence of moral behaviour. It is not that the personality or destiny of a man is the cause of every action, for we saw that personality and destiny are not fixed quantities in any moment of a living man. They exist just because they are built up. They are fixed only when a man is dead and can act no more.

To say that personality is 'the cause' of human actions would put personality above the action and deny liberty and decision. Personality is nothing but action, the action is only an expression of personality.

Today there is a tendency to confuse matters and to speak of moral motivation as if it were the same as causation. Each decision is due to many motives, as each natural happening to many causes. But whilst you can judge of the result of causation by weighing causes against causes, you cannot weigh motives. Since a moral action is the action of a rational being, it results from a decision taken with a regard to motives, but not *due* to them. To put it otherwise: a natural effect is the outcome of the balance of some isolated causes as against other isolated causes; a human action is the result of a pattern of motives. Although motives are (as natural causes are) independent of the human will, the pattern is due to man's mind, is a logical pattern and not a mere weighing of one motive against another. In exactly identical conditions we see two stones acting in the same way; in exactly identical conditions we see two men acting in different ways—just because for both men two times two is four always. The same set of motives cannot form the same pattern in two different minds which have passed through personal (and therefore different) experiences and which have formerly acted in different ways. If for one of them 2 times 2 is four, for the other 2 times 3 *must* be six.

The biographer does not know anything beyond the actions done, which were the results of motivation. He does not know motives and intentions, concealed as these are in the depth of another soul; he knows human actions only in their external effects as natural phenomena. Yet he can elicit the overall effect of the many actions of a man. This is a moral pattern, not because the biographer is able to see directly the unique personality from which it arose, but because the mind of the biographer, being rational, is able to build a logical pattern of several actions. He does not interpret the actions by retracing their causes, as the scientist interprets natural phenomena. But as this general pattern, this destiny or personality, is intimately connected with the pattern of motivation (the intentions and purposes underlying each single action) the biographer can even formulate an explanation, or rather an interpretation of each single action so as to reach a sort of knowledge *à rebours* of the concealed intents of another man.

A doubt may yet arise. If the biographer starts from known events and data, does not biography depend on incidents of which there may be no record? How can it then be maintained that biography is a sound, rationally valid knowledge? We know tolerably well (by reports of contemporaries, documents, etc.) the facts of some lives, and may even be able to distinguish in them what was due to a decision and what was impersonal action, reflex, etc., because the latter are monotonous and repetitive whilst conscious acting shows a certain amount of variety. But we do not have the same extensive knowledge of everybody's life. There are a number of nondescript personalities, humble people whom nobody cared to observe and to report about, who yet were personalities no less than the outstanding ones whom we know from plentiful documents and reports. But this difference does not alter the nature of biography. As a matter of principle, a biography of anybody is possible because everybody is (or may be) a personality. It is only owing to external reasons (lack of data) due to contingent causes that biography sometimes cannot be written.

It might still be maintained that the soundness of a biography is proportional to the amount of data available, although degrees of soundness in biography seem an absurdity. Either it is sound or it is not. But in fact the relative amount of data gives biography more or less *chances* to be sound. When the amount is so small that no rational pattern emerges, biography is not possible. If the amount is comparatively small it may happen that the available data seem to fit into a scheme only owing to coincidence—not because they belong to a logical scheme but because they fit together mechanically. If we should ever learn more facts we would perceive that the pattern we have formed is not a biography. A sufficient amount of data reduces the chance of mistaking casual coherence for a logical pattern, and therefore it is easier and 'safer' to write the biography of a distinguished and therefore documented personality. But any biography is sound when its pattern is logical. There cannot be a wrong logical pattern. There can be a mechanical construction instead of a biographical interpretation, a puppet-show instead of life. And very often the apparent logicality of mechanical coherence will be dissolved without the need of further data, only by trying to give real depth to the interpretation of a few known facts.

Is it possible to attain the innermost truth in studying and describing a life in which the universality of reason and the peculiarity of personality are inextricably blended together? A comparison with history may show where the difficulty of biography lies.

A historical event is an individualized fact. In biography any action of man is already individual, is that one and not another, because it belongs to a certain pattern, to a personality. Instinctive actions, actions due to physiological or environmental causation, etc. can be studied scientifically or individualized historically. But whenever there is the least suspicion of freedom, whenever an action seems to arise from the personality of the agent, that action is already individual and belongs already to a pattern. In other words: actions due to a free decision cannot be considered as such by the historian, because he has to fit the actions of many individuals into an abstract historical pattern. Free decisions instead are already fitted into a real pattern differing from one man to another and constituting a personality.

Any single action does not show by and in itself its quality of being a free action: freedom is revealed only by the logical coherence of several actions. Therefore by individualizing any action whatever the historian denies even the possibility of original coherence. He does not deem it possible that a pattern could exist in the very actions of any individual *before* the historian has invented *his* historical pattern. To put it briefly: he does not take into account that man may be a free agent.

Thence arise the vagaries of idealistic and materialistic historicism, according to which an action cannot possibly be due to a free decision. Its motivation must result from the general pattern of the times in which it was done. Any man (in a certain epoch, and belonging to a certain

social class, etc.) could not but act as he does—because
the historian looks at actions insofar as they fit, or as he
makes them fit (by individualizing them) into a pattern
common to the actions of many men. The historian indeed disregards human freedom far more than the behaviourist and the psychoanalyst do. This is the final
reason for the depraving influence of historicism on public
and private morality. Historicism teaches that the individual is irresponsible. It is therefore quite useless on our
part to think as a rational being should think, and to have
regard to eternal laws in our decisions. On the contrary,
it is almost our duty to try and act as others do, avoiding
any personal decision. Better to follow than to walk
alone—alone in the awful loneliness of being responsible
for anything we do, which means being responsible for
ourselves.

It might seem that history is only a summary of biographies, but it is just the contrary. Historical events refer
to human actions, are human actions, but they are de-
personalized because they are individualized from the
standpoint of a historical pattern. 'Biographical history'
is nonsense—it would imply that it is possible to disregard personality by considering, one by one, actions
taken from their personal context, and at the same time
to take into account personality also, as if it had not been
dissolved by regarding it as a bundle of actions without a
common pattern!

But how can the biographer know and describe another
personality? Are we not bound to an abstract historical
consideration of man? Can we know man's actions other
than as natural events, de-personalized, obvious and
meaningless? To be able to answer these questions, we
must take up again the problem of the knowledge or
'comprehension' of other individuals (discussed already
in Chapter IV) and prove that we can be sure that there
are other men, other personalities besides ourselves. How

can we know that another being is a rational being as we are, when we see only the external side of him and cannot possibly enter into his soul? Is my neighbour a man? Is there, besides me, any other human being?

This is perhaps the most puzzling problem of philosophy. Philosophers worry about the reality of the external world and ask themselves whether, starting from one's own awareness of oneself, it is possible to establish the reality of the world, of what appears to be outside one's consciousness. But it is a far more troublesome problem, whether from one's own consciousness one can reach any certainty that there is some other consciousness besides oneself—that there are other men.

This problem is inextricably involved with the problem of the extent of our own consciousness, of our knowledge of ourselves. If nobody else can, even theoretically, know myself better, more deeply and intimately than I know myself, then I would be completely closed up in myself. One should deny that God himself may know more about myself than I know, and assert that, at least as to myself, my knowledge is as perfect as God's own knowledge is. That is, that I am like God as to myself, or rather that there is no God, if by 'God' I mean something higher than I, with some knowledge of and therefore some power over myself. On the other hand I am a perfect personality and universal reason, a unique being which has universal meaning, all-embracing thought concentrated in a single consciousness. How could its knowing be insufficient or deficient in and by itself?

Human thought, in fact, despite all its power and potential extent, works within a paramount limitation. This is evident when we consider in what manner our minds may conceive universal statements and principles. To our minds this universality seems *to happen*. Logical universality and necessity are for us attributes of a se-quence of conceptions—are shown by the compact course of a logical argument. When one has thought: 'two times two . . . ', one must think *afterwards*: ' . . . is four'. But from the standpoint of pure logic ' . . . is four' is already included in 'two times two'. We conceive this unity as a necessary con-sequence. We say indeed: 'This follows from that. . . . ' But in fact a necessary conclusion, if necessary, is already contained in its premises. Our logic, the logic of our reason, is true logic, universal and necessary logic—but it is 'stretched out' as a sequence of successive statements or steps in time. What in itself is inclusive unity, appears to us as a necessary sequence. But if no unity was there, no sequence would have the character of necessity. We could go on from given premisses to any conclusion if the conclusion was not there already, in the premises.

Our first, paramount limitation is that we are conscious of ourselves in successive moments. Our reason 'remains' the same. It is not one, it is not steadfastly 'there'. Our very personality, therefore, is consciousness and power in each single moment of time and is not given once for ever. It is personality lived through our everydays. When death ends our time, we are not 'changed' but realized as beings beyond time. We shall not become 'something rich and strange'. We are already a rich, strange variety which appears monotonous because only one of the facets of our personality can appear to ourselves at each moment. The unity of these facets, our personality as fixed by death is something exceptional, new, never seen before, which will never exist again—a hard diamond that nobody can ever break up into a meaningless dust of moments.

It is just the everyday quality of our consciousness of ourselves that by its unsufficiency and defectiveness obliges us to reach beyond ourselves and to believe in the existence of something else—of *somebody* else. Our very conception of reality implies indeed the existence of somebody else. My own awareness that I see, say, a tree is bound up with the possibility that another man, in my place, would see the tree. The distinction between dream and fact, fancy and direct sensation, illusion and reality refers to the presumptive existence of another being like myself. A delusion is something which cannot be perceived by another man in my place. Reality means some sensation any other human being would experience should he be in my place.

This means that our conception of reality as something directly known implies an insufficiency of our own thought about reality. Without a prospective confirmation on the part of another human being we could not even think about reality. We could not even distinguish in our very mind between reality and illusion. Our everyday consciousness in itself cannot reach beyond itself to the existence of something else. A presumptive second consciousness is necessary to enable us to state something about reality.

Therefore the universality of our reason (which properly speaking is only the enduring permanence of a certain truth—'two times two is four' is 'steadily and continuously' true) becomes an infinite capacity for repetition. We think it true 'every time' we think of it. Logical universality appears to us stretched out in time because our reason 'goes over' from one to another moment. On the other hand, this everydayness implies a limitation in the extent of our own thought, and therefore we are not immediately conscious of the absolute universality of truth but only of the fact that any other man must think the same. 'Universality' comes to signify 'common to all men'.

It is because of this that the limitation of our thought and the existence of other minds are bound together. The quality of blended universality and individuality of my mind implies the existence of other minds. An existence which seems indeed, at this point, more hypothetical than real—a presumption, not a direct knowledge of a 'thou'. But it is otherwise when one considers rational universality in the field of moral conscience.

Moral acting, in itself, does not prove that another being is a moral and therefore a rational being. When we see the actions of another, we do not see his intentions. An action may be due to moral or immoral motivation, may be instinctive and yet appear the result of a rational decision. From an external point of view we can judge whether the action of another man conforms to, follows moral laws, but not whether it is due only to a respect for moral law. The man we see refraining from killing under great provocation, may refrain because it is written: 'Thou shalt not kill'—but he may even refrain out of fear of the police. Likewise, we are unable to know whether a man, physically made as we are made, is a moral being, endowed with reason and conscience, or an animal, or a mere robot.

But we know (to a certain extent) our own intentions, and know that the universal quality of our reason makes us think, when we act morally, that anybody else should act as we act. Now acting (or deciding to act) does not remain closed up in ourselves, as mere thought does. Our thinking is valid in itself. The belief that any other rational being in our place would think as we think, does not imply that another rational being really exists. Only when we *act*, we imply the *real* existence of some other moral being. And indeed moral actions are not directed to the material world—we cannot be either moral or immoral in our behaviour towards a stone or a tree. It may be wrong to destroy a tree because this deprives other men of its shade and fruits. But towards the stone and the tree and the earth and the stars, in and by themselves, we have no duty.

If, then, there is any moral acting, if our sense of duty and responsibility is not an illusion (and then even the universality of our thought would be an illusion) other human beings must really exist. When we act morally—nay, even when we deliberate whether to do this rather that that on moral grounds—we are in presence of some other human being.

Up to this point we have posited 'another' human being, but only as a consequence of our knowledge of the universal. We know there are other beings bound as we are by valid laws. This does not yet imply the possibility of a knowledge of individuals. Logic, even language and words are a subject of *general* knowledge. Our own individual sensations on the contrary cannot be communicated to any other man save by analogy and inference. It seems therefore impossible to know a particular personality which should be at the same time particular and universal.

But we are free agents, and it is just the absolute liberty of our own will that enables us to understand particular actions. When we see or know of an action of Somebody, we cannot know how Somebody reached the decision. But as it is a human action, we can easily imagine this action as having been done by ourselves and think ourselves (our thought is universal) into the state of mind of deciding to do it. Just because we are free, we can realize in our own mind a variety of motivations for a single action done by another. Were we not free, we could only think of a single possible motivation for it, and this would be causation as in the case of a natural happening.

The same liberty which allows us to choose amongst many motives for our own actions, allows us to represent unto ourselves many possible motivations of an action by another man. Imagination enables us to reproduce the external conditions in which another man acted, moral freedom allows us to realize different motivations to which his acting might have been due. It allows us to realize even non-human causes (natural necessity, heredity, previous conditioning, etc.) to which an action may be due, because, even if they were unconscious causes of the action of another, we can think them, since we are free either to follow them blindly or to resist them in our own acting.

The point of view of the psychoanalyst who denies freedom is inconsistent. He holds that our motivation is due to our submerged ego. But when the unconscious, by clashing against the conscious, produces mental troubles, he advises us to render conscious, i.e. human, our unconscious and not vice versa. The very fact that the healer can appeal to conscious motives against the dark urge of the subconscious proves that human will is free even in regard to unconscious forces. Only a lack of mental activity or a misdirection of it—and mental activity is a choice due to and directed by a moral decision—makes man a prey to instinct. Our first duty as rational beings is to bring reason to bear on everything, and particularly on our soul and life.

Potential awareness of the unconscious is one of the many aspects of our freedom. Everybody can imagine the possible reasons of the actions of another man not only with regard to their conscious motivation but also to their unconscious causation. Even from this latter point of view, the consciousness of the biographer regarding the actions of his subject may be more extensive than the everyday consciousness of the subject himself.

This, however, concerns only the general problem involved in biographical knowledge. We have stated that biography is possible because other human beings besides ourselves exist, and because a particular knowledge of any possible motivation and individual action is possible. But a subject of biography is not *any* human being. His actions are not actions with any kind of human motivation. We have yet to prove that it is possible to know another man as a personality, i.e. as a personal pattern of motivation.

Actions, the pattern of their motivation, and the pattern of a personality are one and the same. The problem therefore is not (as the problem of the historian is) to make several actions fit into the pattern. The pattern is already implied in the motivation of a single action. Personality is not a succession of isolated actions, but a unity. How then can the biographer understand and describe a personality if he himself, as a man, is incapable of describing in full his own personality? This is the question. The biographer can explain the motivation of a single action provided he knows the general pattern of a personality; on the other hand he can know the general pattern because he is able to realize the motivation of the several actions. How is this possible?

A man does not see the general pattern of his own acts because he is not a fixed something—he flows as time flows. The biographer does not depend upon time, is not compelled to flow with the life he describes because he looks at it from beyond it. He is free to choose either to follow (in his own time) the succession of the actions of his subject—or to consider them as a closed circle, as a whole, which is all present to the biographer in a single moment of the biographer's own life.

The first attitude is obviously possible. It seems hardly possible however to know the life of another as a whole. How can one know and describe personality if no overall notion of our own personality is present in our consciousness? On the other hand, how can personality, absolutely unique in itself, be known and described except through some general conception, which by its generality cannot account for such an individual thing as a personality is?

Our mind knows the particular only through the general. When we perceive something, this something is absolutely unique. Even two very similar leaves of grass are more or less different if they are *two* leaves of grass. What we really see is a thing apart, different from everything else. How can we say we know it, if knowing means connecting, understanding, i.e. comparing and finding differences and similarities? Even our recognition of a leaf of grass as 'a leaf of grass' implies something general —the conception of what 'a leaf of grass' is. Kant expressed this drastically by saying that (particular) perception without (general) conception is blind (it is not knowing) whilst a conception without perception is empty. Explanations for this strange situation in our sensory knowledge have been offered in plenty—it is indeed one of the greatest problems of philosophy. But it is not necessary here to decide it one way or another. We can well remain *au dessus de la mêlée* and note only that all philosophers agree that our knowledge of the individual implies a general knowledge too, even if 'general' and 'particular' are not opposed as two completely different worlds, as Plato's ideas and sensations.

In the same way only by reference to some general principle can a particular moral action be known, can, that is, be a conscious, a responsible action. The agent indeed refers it to a moral law, and (as was said above) morality is just this blend of particular act and general law.

But the knowledge of an action on the part of the biographer derives from a quite different generality—from a general scheme of similar actions, as the knowledge of a leaf of grass implies a general conception of many leaves of grass. The difference between knowledge of a particular action on the part of the subject of a biography and on the part of the biographer arises from the fact that the subject sees his action as a future action (he is responsible because his action may happen but has not yet happened) and the biographer sees instead the same action as a past action, irretrievably done.—This is the reason why the biographer is not called on to pronounce a moral judgment on his subject's character and actions. His standpoint cannot be that of a judge because the generality to which he refers particular actions is not a civil or moral law to be followed eventually, but a general scheme of actions already done.

Personality, if general when referred to particular actions, is in itself individual because it is a unity. It is unrepeatable, as a sensation is. A perception, however, is known by reference to general laws of experience. Individual personality cannot be referred to a general rule. On the other hand, we can know an individual thing only by means of some general conceptions. The problem is, which kind of general conception can be brought to bear on personality without destroying its individuality?

We have seen that personality and the several actions of the individual are interdependent. Now, although we cannot think of a personality as a case of some general law, we can form a general conception of a certain kind of *actions* which can be perceived in the external world. Call this general conception 'moral type'. At bottom, a moral type (as it refers to actions done, i.e. to real events and not, like a moral law, to actions not yet happened) is a general conception just as 'leaf of grass', 'tree', 'horse' are. It is different only because it is a conception referring to particular events in so far as they are due to human decisions. When we see a man acting and want to give expression to the relation between the action and the agent, we say that he acts 'like a hero', 'like a miser', etc., or that the action is heroic, avaricious, etc. 'Virtues' and 'vices', the 'habits' of Aristotelian jargon, are types of moral acting. 'The hero', 'the miser', 'the egotist' are classifications of personalities, i.e. they are models, abstract examples of personalities built up by supposing a theoretical type of man whose actions are always due to a single kind of motivation.

A description of moral types was presented in Theophrastus' *Characters*. But they were appreciated rather for their literary elegance and psychological insight than for their speculative implications. These celebrated *Characters* were written in times when theatrical productions were in fashion, and have some relation with the theatre. Comedy proper, the comedy of Menander and

Plautus (and Molière), was not indeed a satirical representation of some real individual (as Aristophanes' plays
were) but rather a reduction of characters to the naked
bones of their personality. Ben Johnson's famous plays
*Every Man in His Humour* and *Every Man Out of His
Humour* (and 'humour' then meant precisely 'character'
in the proper sense, the peculiar bent of somebody's
feelings and doings) show what the platform of comedy
properly is—clashes and mockeries and strange events
arising from the meeting of different types of mankind,
or from a perfectly characterized being (one cannot call
it a 'man') acting amongst real men in our common, real
world.

In his study of the comic Bergson maintained that
laughter arises when we see a man acting mechanically
and not spontaneously. He gives as an example Molière's
avaricious Harpagon replying mechanically, again and
again, to anything the servant is reporting about Harpagon's son being kept a prisoner in a galley and held up
to ransom: 'But why did he go on board that galley?' It
was a fixed idea which kept arising in his mind, when he
should have listened to the circumstances of his son's
misadventure. But Bergson fails to realize that Harpagon
is an example of the general scheme of comedy in the
classical sense. It is indeed the representation of a moral
type confronted with real, distinctive personalities and
with the complexities of life. Therefore comedy is not
always funny. It may well be earnest. The clash between
puppets and real men may sadden the spectator. Comedy
is funny (said Aristotle) only because the vices represented
are of little weight and not destructive as they are in a
tragedy. A superficial distinction is that comedy has a
happy ending, which tragedy has not. But the real distinction is that the 'characters' of comedy are embodi-
ments of moral types whilst those of tragedy are peculiar
personalities.

Both tragedy and comedy have to do with morals. Not

(as Aristotle seems to think) because they teach a moral lesson, but because their characters are either moral types or personalities, and personality, good or bad, can be represented only as a moral conception. Greek tragedy was indeed meant to show how a transgression against the general laws of the cosmos, against 'opportunity', fatally overshadows and brings to ruin the individual through the very action of his own free will. Oedipus and Orestes and Hippolytus ruined themselves because some initial error had irretrievably distorted their judgment, their personality. A character of a Greek tragedy is a human character, it is personality represented as a destiny.

Characters of comedy, on the contrary, are types of possible personalities, theoretical characters. Theophrastus and La Bruyère analysed mere puppets taken from the stage and ranged one alongside the other. Their characters did not act in the pseudo-real world of the stage, but were summaries of actions which could be generalized so as to form an abstract conception of a certain moral type:

It is clear that mistrust (wrote Theophrastus) is a suspicion of wrongdoing on the part of anybody and the mistrustful man is one who when he has sent a servant shopping, sends after him another servant to ask the shopkeepers what prices they charged. And when he has in his pocket a sum of money, he stops eight times in a mile to take it out and count it again. And when he is already in bed, asks his wife whether she locked the strongbox and whether the door has been bolted. . . .

And again:

Wrong refinement (wrote La Bruyère) of taste and character is such only because it is false or feigned, as Emily who cries out loudly at a peril which does not frighten her really; as another girl who blenches at the sight of a mouse only to make herself interesting; or another who pretends to like violets and to swoon when she smells a tuberose.

The contrast between moral type as a generalization of some sides of certain personalities, and personality as

L

destiny can be seen clearly when comedy and tragedy are blended. Look for instance at the fatal personality of King Lear put into tragical relief by the presence of a character of comedy like the Fool, or the meeting of Falstaff and Prince Hal on the stage. Prince Hal makes you laugh because he means to do it—he could act in a quite different way. His personality remains the same both when he is Prince Hal and when he is King Henry V, but his actions are not characterized as those of Falstaff are. Falstaff as a captain is still Falstaff, a mechanical puppet. A puppet, of course, which is not moved by ropes but by a single internal spring—by the one-sided motivation of a Falstaffian abstract type.

Moral types do not really exist, both because no man acts consciously always, and because no two motivations are identical. The personality of a miserly man is not his being a miser but his peculiar way of being a miser, just as this leaf of grass is not *the* leaf of grass but a peculiar object which may be considered as similar to other leaves of grass.

The biographer cannot 'typify' his subject because moral types are rather types of actions than types of personalities. Moral types may help the biographer to understand his subject, but types are general abstract conceptions and therefore are not sufficient to explain the real individuality of a living man.

Let us look closer at the method of Theophrastus and of any description of moral types. They suppose certain situations (say, a man buying in the market-place or meeting a friend) and ask: What would a man do if he was impelled only by avarice? or only by the wish to be tactful and pleasant? A succession of such arbitrarily chosen everyday events and typical human reactions to them allows Theophrastus and 'character'-writers to describe avarice and officiousness as types of human acting. The biographer cannot choose. He is confronted by events which really happened and by a personality which is not

animated by a single type of motivation. But the events
of the life of a man are still a bundle of events, only
loosely bound together by their being events and actions
in the life of somebody. How is the biographer able to
connect them into biographical unity?

The biographer knows moral types, corresponding to
his standard-judgments on actions which, be it remembered, can be judged only as actions and not in their
innermost intention. We are always saying that this
would be a heroic deed, that an avaricious deal, another
a generous action, etc. Therefore from amongst the
actions of his subject the biographer is able to distinguish
a certain number which may be classified as those of a
certain moral type. This is a first generalization—the
first thinking (as opposed to direct or indirect perception
of facts) of the biographer about the life of his subject.
In a sense, the individual and the universal already begin
to coincide at this stage. A biographical pattern begins to
be seen 'as in a glass, darkly'. It is still a dim, twisted
reflection of the pattern of that personality, of that
destiny:

> There is a kind of character in thy life
> That to the observer doth the history
> Fully unfold.

But other actions of the same man seem instead to
belong to other moral types, or a certain action may seem
typical only in a restricted sense. Then the miser, the
hero begin to be more real and less typical. Presently
they are understood as a peculiar miser, a peculiar hero
because there is something (the conception of a determinate type of moral acting) by which to judge of similarities and differences.

To understand the attitude of the biographer one might
compare the characterization of a moral type as done by
Theophrastus, etc., to a construction in a straight line,
one typical event after another. The constructive line of

a biography however in any of its sections is curvilinear and shows that 'bending' which will ultimately close up in a circle the course of a life. The overall representation of a life as a completed circle is not a single general conception. It cannot be because it is something individual, and a moral type is not individual.

In describing a life the biographer has to use singular events, as did Theophrastus when characterizing types of behaviour. But the biographer thinks the events together as a unity, and not as a unitary abstract conception, i.e. as a moral type.

It is indeed a kind of knowing which is different both from our conceptual knowledge of sensorial events and from the abstract construction of moral types. Therefore biography is a paramount science, more truthful in its rendering of reality than scientific generalization and historical individualization can ever be. Telling of events and actions in somebody's life in their temporal succession (the biographer must tell them in this way because he deals with real events which happened in the time-sequence of the life of his subject) the biographer yet evades their everydayness, the temporal thraldom of his subject who experienced each event *after* another event. The biographer can indeed juxtapose two events of his subject's life, disregarding their place in the time-sequence. Just because every action of the subject has already been done, any of his actions can be taken out of their time-sequence and compared to any other. An action and the sequence of actions as they happened in a life which now is concluded, do not run simply forwards, towards a nondescript future. They run towards a *certain* future, towards other specific actions. What I do now, is done towards a blank future. It may be followed by any one of an infinite number of events and actions. When life is finished, however, each action is related to a certain further action, a certain point in the field of the future. The biographer reads any action as a constituent part of a coherent statement, of a clause definitely closed by the full stop of death. It is the conclusive quality of the birth-death clause which is personality and destiny, and gives significance even to casual happenings because they elicited or might have elicited a moral decision of that personality.

One might even maintain, somewhat paradoxically, that the biographer proves he has reached full comprehension of his subject when he is able to say: 'In this case, this individual did not act as might have been expected of him.' It is not a sign of incapacity (or of the impossibility of biography) but a token that the biographer really understands his man. If the biographer is perfectly honest in saying it, it means he has reached the stage when a life is a destiny. A clear-cut destiny, but so personal, so individual that even a sound definition of it must perforce, at this or that moment, fail. This failure puts the seal of authenticity on a biography.

Knowledge of man is paramount knowledge:

> Know then thyself, presume not God to scan,
> The proper study of mankind is man.

But it must be knowledge of man as he really is, of man as an individual absolutely different from any other man. Biography is a theory of man and a method for the description of man directly opposed to any kind of existentialism. No such vague terms as 'worry', or 'horizon', or 'being together' reach the bedrock of existence. Existence is being one's self, not just existing. True existentialism should be biographical insight into another soul as a soul endowed with the exceptional gift of a moral will, of responsibility.

This does not imply that biography can be used as a moral lesson to teach some virtue. One cannot ask the biographer for a judgment on human actions because he does not refer them to a general law but sees them in a personal pattern. Biography teaches only the paramount importance of conscious acting, of rational activity. It teaches that we are building up ourselves and our destiny so long as we live. By impressing on us a vivid sense of our responsibility it may check the debasing influence of history and existentialism which teach that our actions are unavoidable results of the trend of our times, or floating bubbles on a muddy pond of vague worry.

Moreover, in being a study of reality, an effort to connect one's own soul and moral universality, biography has a religious purport. When the task of a biographer is truly performed, personality and destiny, liberty and necessity meet, as Milton emphasized:

> But he that hides a dark soul and foul thoughts,
> Benighted walks under the midday sun:
> Himself is his own dungeon.

Biography seems indeed to be a possible answer to the eternal query: how can I be saved and redeemed only by God's grace if my actions and my judgment lie in my own hands? and how can I be responsible for myself and for my actions if I am good or bad, predestined to be saved or condemned by an inscrutable decree of the Almighty? Such queries are forbidden indeed—and absurd.

> Thou wilt say then unto me: why does He yet find fault? For who has resisted His will?
> Nay but, O man, who art thou that repliest against God? Shall the thing formed say to Him that formed it: Why hast Thou made me thus?
> Hath not the potter power over the clay, of the same lump to make one vessel unto honour and another unto dishonour?

But the doubt beats again and again at the doors of our troubled soul. The vessel, the instrument turns towards its Maker and asks, again and again. The doubt is poignant because God's decree appears as a haunting doom in our life, so that we do not seem to be able to move freely. Only when biography has proved that liberty and destiny flow harmoniously from one another, the contrast no longer appears tragic and we may begin, dimly, to

understand how God can work to His ends through our
freedom, how our freedom may be the expression of the
'unsearcheable dispose of Highest Wisdom'. We may
reach a sort of uneasy peace with the world and its
innermost reasons.

When biographical conscience is lacking, it is either we
or He. Either unlimited freedom, and we are like gods,
knowing and creating good and evil. Or we walk in a
smug assurance of God's grace, and cannot even contemplate the possibility of being in the wrong. In both ways
we stand condemned.

Biography gives pause to our pride before God. Or if
this is too much to be asked from man, biography may at
least give us a sound consciousness of our liberty which is
in itself a limitation. Knowing that our destiny is forged
by our own hands, we may be helped to help ourselves.
At least we may be discouraged from making ourselves a
social nuisance either by disregarding the claims of
morality, or by preaching our own standards as ultimate
truths.

We know indeed that there is something in ourselves
beyond ourselves—a hand stretched out to grasp timeless
existence, ultimate destiny.

# BIBLIOGRAPHICAL NOTE

THIS ESSAY might easily appear to be a hasty exposition of more or less brilliant, irresponsible paradoxes. Nevertheless, it is a unified survey of ideas on history and anthropology that have been expounded severally and justified by more technical procedures in the course of almost thirty years of philosophical research. The author thinks it only fair to the reader and to himself to support his statements by quoting here his previous writings in which the ideas of this essay have been maintained, and to give the exact reference to those works of greater and lesser thinkers to which allusion is made. As these references are meant to justify the author's assessment of the teaching of other thinkers and to enable the reader to check his assertions, the original texts only as known to and used by the author are quoted, even when English translations of foreign works are available.

The now forgotten name of Theodor Lessing had to be put on the first page of this book. He was, indeed, the first thinker who dared to expound a scepticism on the reality of history and the truth of histories as radical as the scepticism evolved by the author of this essay. Before him, earnest but partial doubts had already been expressed in the latter years of the 19th century which was known as 'the century of history'. Lessing's *Geschichte als Sinngebung des Sinnlosen* (history gives a meaning to what does not have any meaning in itself: see pp. 20-21) was published in 1919. About fifteen years later Lessing was forced to escape from Germany into Czechoslovakia, then an independent country. But he was pursued there and murdered by emissaries of Hitler who believed in the absolute truth of history and who used it as a justification of his tyranny.

CHAPTER I takes up again the main ideas of a course of lectures given at the University of Bologna, 1931-32 (see the inaugural lecture, 'Motivi antistoricistici', *Rivista di psicologia*, 1931) and of the essay 'Esiste la storia?', *Nuova Rivista Storica*, 1940. — The landscape-theory (p. 27) has been expounded in full in 'Appunti sul paesaggio', *Annuario Lic. Sc. Forlì*, 1930.

On historicism in general, too many books should be quoted here, but Meinecke's *Die Entstehung des Historismus*,

1936 (see the author's review in *Nuova Rivista Storica*, 1937) must be mentioned as a general and most authoritative text — p. 4f: ref. to Bacon's *De Augmentis*, to Bossuet's *Discours sur l'histoire universelle*, to St. Augustine's *De civitate Dei* — p. 5ff: see Vico's *La Scienza Nuova*, 1725 a.o. and cp. Croce's *La filosofia di G. B. Vico*, 1911 — p. 10: quotation from Croce's *La storia come pensiero e come azione*, 1937 — p. 10: quotations from Lorenz's *Geschichtswissenschaft*, Nietzsche's *Ueber die Zukunft unserer Bildungsanstalten* (see also *Vom Nutzen und Nachteil der Historie für das Leben*) and Troeltsch's *Der Historismus und seine Ueberwindung*, 1924 — p. 11: on the feeble development of British historicism in the 19th century, see K. Dockhorn, *Der deutsche Historismus in England*, 1950, and cp. the author's note, 'La filosofia della storia in Granbretagna', *Nuova Rivista Storica*, 1952 — p. 12: ref. to Mach's *Analyse der Empfindungen*, 1900, and to Whitehead's *The Concept of Nature*, 1920 — p. 14: ref. to Eddington's *The Nature of the Physical World* — p. 15: see Rickert's *Kulturwissenschaft und Naturwissenschaft*, 1915³, and Windelband's *Geschichte und Naturwissenschaft*, 1904³ — p. 22: ref. to St. Augustine's *Confessions*, X and *De Gen. co. Man.* — p. 23: ref. to Bergson's *Données immédiates* and *Durée et simultanéité* — p. 24: ref. to Croce's *Teoria e storia della storiografia*, 1917, Ch. I; and to Gentile's *Sistema di logica*, 1918, II — p. 24: see Comte's *Cours de phil. pos.*, Feuerbach's *Das Wesen des Christentums*, Hegel's *Encyklopädie*, §555, etc. — p. 25: quotation from Hegel's *Geschichtsphilosophie*— p. 25ff: Spengler's *Untergang des Abendlandes*, 1918-22 — p. 31: ref. to Manzoni's essay *Del romanzo storico*, 1845.

CHAPTER II—A strictly *logical* scepsis against the concept of 'history of philosophy' will be found in the author's 'La verità come problema logico', *Studi filosofici*, Milan, III. 3 (1942) — The development of philosophical thought as 'problematicism' (see p. 42) had formerly been enforced by the author himself in his book, *Per una concezione attivistica della filosofia*, 1927 — The author's conception of modern philosophy is a development of ideas expressed by Husserl in Parts I and II of 'Die Krisis der europäischen Wissenschaften und die transzendentale Phänomenologie' in *Philosophia*, Belgrad, 1936-7 (see review by the author in *Logos*, 1939, p. 680ff): Part III was only published in 1954. This conception was used by the author in his new interpretation of Hobbes' philosophy (*Alle fonti del deismo e del materialismo moderno*, 1942, Part II) and in his final assessment of Berkeley's and Kant's position (*Saggio su Berkeley*, 1955) — The paramount value of logic (p. 64) as against any other consideration is the leading thought in the author's theory of hyper-logic as expounded in his essays published in *Logos* from 1937 to 1944: cf. also p. 143f.

P. 36: ref. to Gentile's essay, *Il circolo di filosofia e storia della filosofia* and to Hegel's *Vorlesungen über die Geschichte der Philosophie* — p. 57f: ref. to Hegel's *Encyklopädie*, § 262ff, and to Schopenhauer's *Wille in der Natur* — p. 58: ref. to Galileo's *Massimi sistemi* — p. 60: ref. to Kant's *Kritik d. r. Vernunft*, Intr. V.2 — p. 64: ref. to Heidegger's *Kant und das Problem der Metaphysik*, 1929.

CHAPTER III—The groundwork of this chapter will be found in the author's essay 'The Golden Age', *Cronos, Quarterly Review of the Ohio State University*, 1947 — As to the theory of Progress, see the essay on 'Etica crepuscolare', *Rivista di psicologia*, 1927 — p. 71: an allusion to the conception of the Renaissance outlined in the essay 'Note sulla modernità del Rinascimento', *Nuova Rivista Storica*, 1950 — for Bacon (p. 78) see *Saggio su F. Bacon*, 1933, Ch. XVI.

P. 69: ref. to Tasso's *Aminta* and his *Dialoghi* — p. 69: M. A. Flaminio is presented by Vida (in his *De rei publicae dignitate*) as an early anarchist, but see the doubts expressed by Toffanin, *L'umanesimo al concilio di Trento*, 1955 — p. 69: Rousseau's early essay, *Discours sur les sciences et les arts*, first intended as an insincere, brilliant paradox, and then insisted on and developed in his further writings — p. 74: ref. to Perry's *Growth of Civilization* and his theory of the origin of war — p. 78: quotation from Bentham's *Principles* — p. 81: ref. to Montesquieu's *Esprit des lois*, and to J. Millar's *Origin of Ranks*; earlier forerunners of Marx could be added here, from Harrington and Petty to many Italian economists of the 18th century — p. 82: the authority as to the 'official' theory of historical materialism and to Lenin's interpretation, is G. A. Wetter's *Il materialismo dialettico sovietico*, 1948.

CHAPTER IV reproduces the main lines of the author's course of lectures on existentialism at the University of Bologna, 1930-31, already summarized in Primo saggio sull'uomo, *Rivista di psicologia*, 1935 — The statements on historic and existentialist 'comprehension' (p. 119ff) refer to the essay: 'Appunti sul problema del comprendere', *Logos*, 1939.

P. 96: quotations from Hegel's *Encyklopädie*, §542 and

§534 — p. 97: Schopenhauer's *Welt als Wille und Vorstellung* was published in 1819 — p. 99: ref. to Fichte's *Bestimmung des Gelehrten* — p. 102: as to Marheineke, the author's authority is K. Barth's *Protestantische Theologie im 19ten Jahrhundert* — p. 102: ref. to Schleiermacher's *Monologien*, Feuerbach's *Dreissig Vorlesungen über das Wesen der Religion* and Strauss' *Voltaire* — p. 107: ref. to Jaspers' *Nietzsche: Einführung in das Verständnis seines Philosophierens*, 1936 (cp. the author's critical note in *Logos*, 1937, as to the connection between Jaspers' existentialism and his interpretation of Nietzsche) — p. 110: ref. to Scheler's *Formalismus in der Ethik*, 1913, and the author's criticism in his *Saggio sul rimorso*, 1933, Ch. I — p. 110: ref. to Husserl's *Vorlesungen zur Phänomenologie des inneren Zeitbewusstseins*, edited by Heidegger in 1928, i.e. a year after the publication of his own *Sein und Zeit* — p. 115: ref. to Misch's 'Lebensphilosophie und Phänomenologie', *Phil. Anz.* 1929-30 — p. 115-6: ref. especially to Jaspers' lectures on *Vernunft und Existenz*, 1935; and for the controversial aspect of Berdyaev's existentialism, to Berdyaev's *Cinq méditations sur l'existence*, 1936 (cp. also Wahl's *Petite histoire de l'existentialisme*, 1952) — p. 118: ref. to Sartre's minor essay, *L'existentialisme est un humanisme*, 1946 — p. 119f: ref. especially to Dilthey's *Kritik der historischen Vernunft* — p. 123: the quotation is taken from a lecture by A. Abbagnano, professor at the University of Turin, Italy — p. 124: on marxist existentialism, see Marcuse's 'Beiträge zur Phänomenologie des historischen Materialismus', *Phil. Hefte*, 1928, and the author's discussion in *Problema del comprendere* quoted above — p. 125: ref. to Stirner's *Der Einzige und sein Eigentum* — p. 127: Koepp's essay was published in a review in 1929 under the title 'Merimna und Agape'.

CHAPTER V—This chapter is a development of theories already presented in the essays: 'Appunti sulla biografia' (*Rivista di psicologia*, 1928) and *Primo saggio sull'uomo* as quoted above — The 'everydayness' of life was used as an introduction to *Swift, or The Egotist*, 1934 — The paramount importance of presumptive 'other' human beings was insisted on in 'Abbozzo d'un esame del concetto di realtà' (*Rivista di psicologia*, 1926), in *Problema del comprendere* quoted above, last part, and in *Lavoratore nell'universo*, 1947, Ch. I. — Here the author follows Kant's moral teaching, with some modifications already expounded in his *Saggio sul rimorso*, 1933 — This theory of biography should explain and justify the author's biographical studies and essays (on Bacon, Berkeley, Herbert of Cherbury, Swift, Voltaire, etc.) and his contention, that biographies (*his* biographies, at least) should be considered not as historical monographies but as explorations in the field of moral philosophy. — As to the religious ideas underlying this and the former chapters (and in particular the relation between history and eschatology and the equivalence of destiny and free will) the author refers to the second part of his *Verso una teologia*, 1946.

P. 152: an allusion to Bergson's *Le rire* — p. 153: see Aristotle's *Poetics*.

_____

The author wishes to thank the delegates of the Edinburgh University Press for the honour of having this work published under the University imprint, and the Secretary of the Press for advice on matters of style.

# INDEX

Abbagnano, A., 123, 163
Abel, 73
Adam, 70, 73, 88
Anaximander, 46
Anaximenes, 46
Aquinas, 38
*Aristotelianism*, 54, 62, 75
Aristophanes, 152
Aristotle, 37-8, 41, 52-4, 59, 95, 152-3, 164
Augustine, 4, 5, 22, 82, 105, 126, 161

Bacon, 4, 38, 78-9, 161, 164
Barth, K., 163
Bentham, 78, 162
Berdyaev, 116, 163
Bergson, 23, 82, 115, 152, 161, 164
Berkeley, 59, 61, 63, 162, 164
Bossuet, 4, 161
Bruno, 56

Caesar, 17
Cain, 73
Cicero, 4, 52
Clement, 55
Comte, 24, 89, 161
Copernic, 57
Copleston, 37
Cordelia, 104
Cordemoy, 61
Croce, 1, 5, 10, 115, 161
Cromwell, 26

Dante, 95
Descartes, 38, 57-61, 98-100, 105, 117, 123

Dicearch, 75
Dilthey, 115, 119
Diodoros Chronos, 52
Diogenes Laertius, 37
Dockhorn, K., 161
Duns Scotus, 38

Eddington, 14, 161
Einstein, 60
*Eleatics*, 47
*Epicureans*, 55
Epicurus, 38
Epimetheus, 88
Eucken, 37

Falstaff, 154
*Fathers of the Church*, 55
Feuerbach, 24, 102, 161, 163
Fichte, 64, 99, 163
Flaminio, M. A., 162

Galileo, 58, 162
Gentile, 36, 161-2
Geulincx, 61
Gibbon, 30
*Gnostics*, 55
Gomperz, 52

Harpagon, 152
Harrington, 162
Harvey, 19
Hegel, 2, 24, 37-8, 57, 64, 94, 96-9, 108, 117, 161-2
*Hegelians*, 82, 102
Heidegger, 64, 110-13, 115-22, 127, 162-3
Henry V, 154
Heraclitus, 38, 47

165

'E DUE